Follow these Writers...

in SUSSEX

A Handbook for Literary Detectives

Judith Bastide and Michael Rich

authorHOUSE®

AuthorHouse™ UK Ltd.
500 Avebury Boulevard
Central Milton Keynes, MK9 2BE
www.authorhouse.co.uk
Phone: 08001974150

First published by AuthorHouse   2011

ISBN: 978-1-4567-7220-8 (sc)

To all our Grandchildren

CONTENTS

INTRODUCTION

Have you ever wished you had a knowledgeable friend who could help you find out more about the places that inspired your favourite writers?

Let this book be that friendly guide around Sussex, along main roads and off beaten tracks, down country lanes and back streets. On the way you'll uncover some fascinating information.

Did you know that in 1881 Lewis Carroll and Karl Marx were both on holiday in Eastbourne at the same time (though not together)? Or that after designing his dream house at Black Down on the Sussex/Surrey border, filled with all the very latest Victorian must-have amenities, Alfred, Lord Tennyson, luxuriated in at least three baths a day? Have you speculated on the reason for Winnie the Pooh's unusual name? The answer will be found in the chapter about The Weald and Ashdown Forest.

Seven major centres in East and West Sussex have been selected and whichever mode of transport you choose - foot, car or bicycle, there's plenty of helpful information here to enrich your investigations. There are suggestions for one day, two day or longer visits. Of course, it's not always possible to indulge oneself. You may be travelling with backseat passengers who are not completely sympathetic to the idea of hunting down famous writers! There are plenty of suggestions in each chapter for child friendly places close to centres of literary pilgrimage and, who knows, this kind of detective work is highly addictive and they may easily succumb.

So whether you are on holiday in Sussex or lucky enough to live there, dip into this book to find out more about the colourful writers who have been inspired by "Good old Sussex by the sea", as Kipling described it.

Enjoy your travels!

BRIGHTON and HOVE

(Not forgetting Rottingdean)

BRIGHTON ROCKS!

Brighton and Hove are not identical twins and both dislike being associated with the other's reputation. Ask any resident of Hove and they will smile slightly apologetically before admitting that they live in "Hove actually".

That word 'actually' acknowledges the rather genteel, even staid, atmosphere the town has sometimes been given. It's not a description that Brighton has had to worry about!

Both glamorous and seedy and popularly known as 'London-by-the-Sea' (the satirical magazine 'Private Eye' calls Brighton 'Skidrow-on-Sea'), Brighton owes its fame to Dr. Richard Russell, originally a resident of nearby Lewes who, in 1753, published 'The Use of Sea Water in Diseases of the Glands'.

For centuries the fishing village of Brighthelmstone had led a life of quiet obscurity. All that changed when the trend setters of the late eighteenth century, including Dr. Johnson and, later, the Prince Regent himself (later George IV), took up Dr. Russell's views and came to the fashionable health spa, now renamed Brighton, to see and be seen.

BRIGHTON'S WRITERS

Hester Thrale (1741-1821) and her Literary Circle

Whilst still living in London, Mrs Hester Thrale and her wealthy husband bought a second home in West Street, Brighton in 1775. For the next ten years this became a centre for writers and intellectuals as Mrs. Thrale hosted glittering literary parties with many of the greatest writers of the day, making the journey here from London.

One of the first, in 1779, to accept the Thrales' invitation was **Fanny Burney (1752-1840)**.

The previous year her novel 'Evelina' had been a sensational success, so much so that she was mobbed when she appeared at Brighton Assembly Rooms. She wrote in her diary: "I shall certainly escape going any more". Amazingly, she much preferred the sea bathing – even in November!

In her diary, a marvellous first hand picture of fashionable Brighton life at the time, she recounts: "We rose at six o'clock in the morn and by the pale blink o' the moon went to the seaside where we had bespoken the bathing-woman to be ready for us, and into the ocean we plunged. I have bathed so often as to lose my dread of the operation".

The description sends a shiver down one's back but the sea bathing did not deter her and for the next ten years she was a frequent visitor.

An even more distinguished visitor was **Samuel Johnson (1709-1784)**.

The lexicographer, critic and poet was a close friend of the Thrales and devoted to "young Burney", his protégée. Here in Brighton he wrote 'The Lives of the Poets' and Hester Thrale corrected the proofs. But although he was surrounded by friends and admirers, he disliked Brighton.

"It is so truly desolate that, if one had a mind to hang oneself for desperation at being obliged to live there, it would be difficult to find a tree on which to fasten the rope" (take no notice of that today - the parks are worth all the time you can spare for them).

In 1781 Henry Thrale died and his widow maintained the house and lavish lifestyle for the next four years. But then there was an unexpected development. She fell in love with Gabriel Piozzi, an Italian singer whom she had met in Brighton. Her daughters, Dr Johnson and Fanny Burney all disapproved but love triumphed.

The Brighton house was sold and the couple married and went to live abroad. Her first marriage had been a loveless affair but second time around she seems to have been blissfully happy.

Rudyard Kipling (1865-1936)

Kipling was thirty two in 1897 and already a famous writer when he returned to England with his American wife and two daughters, finally settling in Rottingdean, three miles east of Brighton.

The pretty village was already home to several of his illustrious relations and initially the Kiplings moved into North End, the holiday home of his uncle, Edward Burne-Jones, the notable painter. A few months later, after Carrie gave birth to their son John, they moved across the village green to The Elms, renting it for three guineas a week.

Rottingdean home of
Rudyard Kipling

Plaque on the wall to record this

On the third side of the village green was The Dene, home of the Ridsdales.

Their daughter married Stanley Baldwin, Rudyard's cousin and the future Prime Minister. Kipling himself commented on this close knit family grouping: "You could throw a cricket ball from any one house to another".

Angela Thirkell, the novelist granddaughter of Edward Burne-Jones, remembered childhood holidays at North End House playing with cousin Ruddy and his daughters.

Life was good. How fortunate they could not see what the future held for their family. It was during the brief Rottingdean years that Kipling completed 'Stalkey & Co' and wrote 'The Just-So Stories' and 'Kim'.

After two happy years all changed as the Kipling family made what turned out to be a tragic return visit to Carrie's family in America. It was mid-winter and there was a stormy Atlantic crossing. When the boat docked in New York the whole family had been taken ill. Kipling had an inflamed lung and the two little girls both had whooping cough.

Kipling himself became so ill that he could not be given the dreadful news that his beloved Josephine, only eight years old, had developed pneumonia which then proved fatal. His remaining daughter Elsie wrote in later life: "His life was never the same after her death; a light had gone out that could never be rekindled".

They returned to Rottingdean with all its reminders of their lost daughter. It was almost more than they could bear and their lives were made even worse as hordes of day trippers came out on double-decker horse-drawn buses from Brighton, trying to catch a glimpse of the famous writer.

The Kiplings needed a fresh start. Finally, in 1902, they found Batemans, a much more secluded house near Burwash and this became their home for the rest of Kipling's life (see the Ashdown Forest chapter for more about his life there).

MORE ROTTINGDEAN RESIDENTS

At least two more famous writers, both women, spent time in Rottingdean, both hoping the sea air would have a beneficial effect on their health.

Katherine Mansfield (1888-1923)

Born Katherine Mansfield Beauchamp, she arrived in March 1910 to lodge above the grocer's shop in Rottingdean. The daughter of the Bank of New Zealand's chairman, she had had a very chaotic personal life prior to her arrival in the village.

The previous year, aged only 21 and recently returned to London, where she had studied earlier, she had married the singer George

Bowden, just three weeks after their first meeting. The bride wore black - not a very promising sign - and then disappeared on her wedding night. There was a brief reconciliation early in 1910 but the marriage was clearly doomed before it began. She was suffering from ill health and had already had an operation for peritonitis. Her close friend, Ida Baker, who knew her from their college days, brought her to Rottingdean to recuperate in mind and body.

Recovery was not immediate but the peaceful respite had its effect. Her energies were restored and a much stronger Katherine, not Beauchamp, not Bowden but now Mansfield emerged, although her subsequent life was continually marked by similar periods of collapse.

Interestingly, although some of her short stories are set in New Zealand, the coastal scenes she describes there could equally well be those she remembered of the Sussex coast and those happy months of calm.

Enid Bagnold (1889-1981)

A bout of ill health also brought Enid Bagnold to Rottingdean in 1923 when she was recovering from a tonsillectomy. On that occasion she stayed with friends at The Grange. The following year she and her husband, Sir Roderick Jones, the Chairman of Reuters, bought North End House, Edward Burne-Jones's former home. Subsequently they also bought The Elms, Kipling's former home and a racing stable in the village.

She had already written two novels but then turned her attention to children's literature, her greatest success being 'National Velvet'. A fourteen year old schoolgirl wins a horse which she then, while disguised as a boy, rides to victory in the Grand National. It is said that the heroine's family was based on that of the Rottingdean butcher, Mr Hilder.

In 1944, nine years after the novel's publication, it was made into a film and it was this which made the twelve year old Elizabeth Taylor world famous. On several occasions surprised Rottingdean residents came face to face with Miss Taylor, who was calling on the writer who had opened the way to stardom for her.

Others were not so appreciative of the novelist's work. Virginia and Leonard Woolf lived ten miles away in Rodmell, outside Lewes (see the Lewes chapter for a much more detailed account of their lives). Leonard

Woolf wrote somewhat harshly to a friend in April 1962: "Last night I went to 'The Chalk Garden' by Enid Bagnold at the Lewes Theatre. The play was even more appalling than 'The Cherry Orchard'".

Although Enid Bagnold died at her London home and was cremated in Golders Green, her ashes were buried in Rottingdean churchyard. A simple wooden plaque on the outside wall close to the church door records that her ashes are there.

Graham Greene (1909-1991)

Graham Greene, an intermittent visitor, will always be closely associated with the city through his hugely successful novel 'Brighton Rock'.

He had first visited Brighton when he was six and then returned as a seventeen year old in 1926, staying opposite the West Pier as he began work on his first published novel, a historical thriller, 'The Man Within'.

Two years later he was back again to prepare an article for The Times: 'A Walk on the Sussex Downs'. By 1936 he was actually living in Clapham when the London newspapers reported trials at Lewes Assizes where the Brighton Racecourse gangs were quashed for ever.

Almost immediately, an intrigued Greene was visiting Brighton to begin his research into the gang warfare. At the same time a sordid local murder also attracted him. When an unclaimed trunk at Brighton railway station was opened it revealed a woman's torso. The popular description of Brighton as 'Queen of the Slaughtering Places' was somewhat harsh but it did give Greene some justification for setting his gruesome story in the city.

John Boulting, who directed the 1947 film version (with a script written by Greene himself, in collaboration with Terence Rattigan), was chiefly attracted to the novel by its strong sense of place. "The setting was not a backdrop, it was one of the characters", he commented.

Amusingly, Greene wrote to his brother shortly after the book's publication: "A new shade of knickers and nightdresses has been named 'Brighton Rock' by Peter Jones. Is this fame?" Not surprisingly, the town's authorities were not happy with the adverse publicity this produced, as Greene also wrote: "It must have galled them to see my book unwittingly advertised at every sweet stall: 'Buy Brighton Rock!'".

He was still not finished with Brighton. Almost thirty years later it featured again in the delightful 'Travels with my Aunt'. The aunt in question, Henry Pulling's Aunt Augusta, liked "to be at the centre of the entire devilry with the buses going off to all those places. She spoke as though their destinations were Sodom and Gomorrah rather than Lewes and Patcham and Littlehampton and Shoreham".

OTHER WRITERS

Ivy Compton-Burnett (1884-1969)

The seventh out of twelve children, this homeopath's daughter was born in Middlesex but the family moved to First Avenue, Hove when she was seven years old and then, six years later, to The Drive.

Her whole childhood was effectively spent in Hove, Brighton's twin resort. She left home to read Classics at Royal Holloway College, London but returned to take over the running of the large and difficult household after her mother's death. Ten years earlier her father had died and her mother suffered severe depression, going into deep mourning for the rest of her life and tyrannising her children. Even the baby was forced to wear black all the time.

If the younger children hoped things would be easier when big sister took up the reins of household management they were in for a very nasty surprise. Like mother, like daughter, Ivy proved as harsh and, some say, as uncaring as her mother.

Matters came to a head during the First World War with a series of family tragedies. In 1916 her beloved brother Noel was killed on the Somme. Even more unbearably, on Christmas Day the following year, her two younger sisters committed joint suicide in their bedroom and then in 1918 Ivy herself was very ill with pneumonia.

She left Hove for London where she lived for thirty two years with Margaret Jourdain, a writer and expert on Regency furniture.

No experience is wasted by a writer and the tensions and difficulties in her own family re-emerge in Ivy Compton-Burnett's novels. All consist largely of dialogue and all, especially the major ones such as 'A Family and a Fortune' and 'Manservant and Maidservant', investigate the difficult tyrannical relationships within dysfunctional families.

Virginia Woolf wrote in her diary that her own writing was "much inferior to the bitter truth and intense originality of Miss Compton-Burnett" and that such thoughts kept her awake at night.

Angela Thirkell (1890-1961)

Grand daughter of Edward Burne-Jones and first cousin to Rudyard Kipling and Stanley Baldwin, Angela Thirkell had a glittering intellectual background.

This continued into the next generation with one of her sons, Colin MacInnes, also becoming a novelist whilst another, Lancelot, became Comptroller of the BBC.

Angela Thirkell becomes part of the Brighton story through her frequent childhood visits to her Burne-Jones grandparents in Rottingdean. Her memories of these visits, especially in her 1931 autobiography 'Three Houses', give a vivid picture of the Edwardian summer. The cousins played Roundheads and Cavaliers together while 'Uncle Ruddy' read the 'Just so Stories' aloud in his "deep, unhesitating voice".

After the breakdown of her second marriage, Angela Thirkell turned to novel writing to support her young family. Her very successful formula, producing over thirty novels, was to take the inhabitants of Trollope's Barsetshire and to document the lives of their descendants.

Her own characters even lived in the same places and shared some characteristics with their imagined forebears. Sussex, however, had played such a seminal role in her young life, that it is very easy to see much of her beloved county in this fictional one.

There was to be a novel a year, which she referred to, in a letter to her editor, as: "new wine in old bottles". She remains a permanent part of Rottingdean. On her death she was buried in the churchyard alongside her infant daughter, Mary.

Patrick Hamilton (1904-1962)

During his lifetime Patrick Hamilton had a high reputation as a novelist and playwright with two great theatrical successes to his name. Sadly, his work has since been neglected and not all is still in print.

Although he published his first novel, 'Monday Morning' in 1925 when he was still only 21, it was his 1929 play 'Rope' which catapulted him to overnight success. This was then followed in 1938 by 'Gaslight', a chilling Victorian drama of a husband's attempt to drive his wife mad to get hold of her fortune. It was twice made into a film with the Hollywood version winning a Best Actress Oscar for its star, Ingrid Bergman.

Hamilton was born over the Downs from Brighton, in nearby Hassocks and knew the city well, even though he spent much of his life in London. His novel 'The West Pier' is set in Brighton with Graham Greene stating: "It is the best book written about Brighton".

Peter James (1948-)

Film producer and crime writer, Peter James was born in Hove (actually!) and still spends part of his time in Sussex as well as some time in Notting Hill. His first real success was in 1988 with 'Possession'.

Of particular interest to Brighton readers is his series of crime novels, beginning with 'Dead Simple', published in 2005 and featuring Detective Superintendent Roy Grace. All are set in Peter James' native Brighton and Hove and it is possible to trace most of the settings of the novels in the real city. Addicts will probably want to do just that, without being side tracked by other writers.

In 1938 his mother, twenty one year old Cornelia Katz, a Jewish glove maker, escaped from the Nazis when they occupied her native Vienna. On arriving in England she met and married Jack James. Her glove making skills were quickly recognised by top couturiers and in 1947 she made the gloves Princess Elizabeth (later Queen Elizabeth) wore on her wedding day.

ONE DAY VISIT

We have assumed that our readers have only limited time to investigate an area, perhaps just a weekend, so in order to see as much as possible our suggested itinerary could feel a little rushed. If you have the luxury of more time, it might be preferable to spread all the sightseeing over a more leisurely two days.

If it is to be one day, make an early start, give up the car and begin at the railway station. Many have said that arriving at the city by train feels as if one is entering by the back door. One emerges to a warren of narrow streets with hardly a glimpse of the sea.

Patrick Hamilton (1904-1962) used the station in his 1941 novel 'Hangover Square' to illustrate the leading character, George Harvey Bone, and his fantasy of escaping from his sordid life in Earl's Court.

Coming out of the station make your way to Queen's Road which becomes West Street and eventually reaches the seafront. On the left hand side is Gloucester Road. The whole area round here features in the film version of **Graham Greene's** 'Brighton Rock' and you should be able to recognise many of the settings.

Continue down Gloucester Road and second on the left is Over Street, where some of the characters in Patrick Hamilton's 1950 masterpiece 'The West Pier' lived.

Continue on Gloucester Road and further down on the left is Tidy Street, the probable home of Cubitt, Pinkie's henchman in 'Brighton Rock'. Cross Gloucester Road and turn right down Kensington Gardens, then cross North Street to Gardener Street. Continue down to the end and at the junction with Church Street turn right.

Take a deep breath and a rather steep walk will bring you to St Nicholas Church. This was the original parish church in Brighthelmstone where you will find a plaque on the north wall to the memory of **Dr. Johnson**, who worshipped here with the Thrale family.

It's downhill now. Turn left down Dyke Road leading back to Queen's Road and on to the Clock Tower, a significant landmark round here. In 'The West Pier', Patrick Hamilton described this as the dividing line between the two very different sides of Brighton: "the bright yet shallow promise of the Front and the crowded squalor of the back streets".

Queen's Road has now become West Street. In the eighteenth century this was the most fashionable road in Brighton but that glory has long given way to a motley collection of shops, family restaurants and amusement arcades.

On your right hand side you will see the impressive exterior of St. Paul's church. At the time of writing there is an empty building opposite it on the left hand side between a Family Leisure Arcade and Revolution Restaurant. Near the end of the building is a single iron post which, possibly uniquely, is listed by the Department of the Environment as a 'building' of architectural and historical interest.

This is all that now remains of **Hester Thrale**'s house, where anyone who was anyone in eighteenth century Brighton would certainly want to be seen. There is a plaque on the wall marking the building and telling of the regular visits of **Dr Johnson** and **Fanny Burney**.

Continue down West Street to the traffic lights. At last you can see the sea.

Brighton has two piers although only one of them, the Palace Pier, is in working order. Turn right along King's Road (it runs beside the sea and in many other cities it would be called The Promenade) towards the West Pier, now closed and fallen into disrepair.

West Pier

Near here is a Holiday Inn which incorporates some of the former Bedford Hotel built in 1829. **Charles Dickens** stayed here in 1847 when he was writing 'Dombey and Son' and put Dombey himself there when he came to see his young son Paul. Dr. Blimber's Academy, young Dombey's school, was based on Chichester House on King's Cliff Parade.

Just beyond the Bedford Hotel was the original site of the garrison for the 10,000 soldiers the town supported after the outbreak of war against France in 1793. **Jane Austen** almost certainly never visited the town but she fully understood its attractions.

In 'Pride and Prejudice' it becomes the place of Lydia's downfall, although "in Lydia's imagination a visit to Brighton comprised every possibility of earthly happiness. She saw the streets of the gay bathing-place covered with officers and seeing herself the object of attention."

Retrace your steps. Preston Street comes off King's Road between the Holiday Inn and Metropole hotels. Number 59 is where Hilda Lessways, the eponymous heroine of **Arnold Bennett's** 1911 second novel in the Clayhanger Quartet, ran a boarding house. The Metropole itself plays a significant part in Patrick Hamilton's 'The West Pier'.

Continue past the Grand Hotel, crossing West Street and King's Road towards the Old Ship Hotel.

Old Ship Hotel

There has been an inn on this spot since the time of Queen Elizabeth I.

Dickens stayed here while he was writing 'Oliver Twist' (1837) and 'Barnaby Rudge' (1841). **William Thackeray** spent some time here in 1847 while writing 'Vanity Fair' and sets some of the most memorable scenes in the novel here, notably Becky Sharp arriving to ruin sweet natured Amelia's honeymoon.

King's Road leads into Grand Junction Road past the Royal Albion Hotel (built in 1826), the site of Dr. Richard Russell's house. There is a plaque on the wall to the memory of the man who popularised Brighton as a spa. Graham Greene stayed here too while researching 'Brighton Rock'. You have seen the view in front of you in so many films including 'Genevieve' (1953), 'Oh What a Lovely War' (1969) and 'Portrait of a Marriage' (1990).

Turn left down Old Steine and you will come to the Royal Pavilion.

Royal Pavilion

William Cobbett (1763-1835) in his 'Rural Rides' wrote of this extraordinary building: "Take a square box and a large Norfolk turnip and put the turnip on top of the box. Then take four turnips of half the size and put them on the corners of the box. Then take a considerable number of bulbs of the crown-imperial and put them pretty promiscuously about the top of the box".

The Prince Regent, later George IV, commissioned John Nash to design him this extravaganza, after first visiting the resort in 1783. Although it was his patronage which directly led to Brighton's fashionable reputation he was not the trail-blazer. Nearly ten years earlier, Hester

Thrale had bought her house in West Street. In fact she left the town in 1785, just as the Prince was moving in but it seems unlikely there was any connection between the two events.

The Pavilion is open to the public and is well worth exploring. If you then make your way along North Street towards the Clock Tower you are in the heart of the shopping and restaurant district. You'll have no problem finding plenty of places to eat and to recover from the morning walking tour.

Well fortified, it's time for the afternoon exploration. If you have now been reunited with your car it's a pleasant ten minute drive eastwards along the A259 coast road to Rottingdean. Alternatively, the Number 2 or 2A buses from stop B on Old Steine will take you there. Today this pretty, quintessentially English, village is a charming retreat from the hustle and bustle of cosmopolitan Brighton but it was not always such a gentle place.

For two hundred years the Rottingdean Gang of smugglers operated here, hiding their contraband in the tunnels which connected the cellars of houses along the High Street. **Kipling** romanticised this in 'A Smuggler's Song'.

Park by the picturesque village green and duck pond and make your way to The Grange, an elegant eighteenth century house on the corner of Vicarage Lane and Whiteway Lane. Inside you'll find the local library, Art Gallery and Museum with one fascinating room in the latter devoted to Kipling memorabilia.

There are first editions of Kipling's books, twenty six of his letters and some excellent prints of the original illustrations in 'The Jungle Book'. A further room deals with his uncle, Edward Burne-Jones. The Grange Museum is open daily 10am to 4pm (although closed on Wednesdays) and 2pm to 4pm on Sundays.

After leaving The Grange, walk down beside the Green to St.Margaret's parish church. This flint church has some Saxon foundations with the inevitable restoration by the Victorians. It is particularly noted for its stained glass windows, seven of which were designed by Burne-Jones and made by William Morris. In the churchyard are the graves of Enid Bagnold and Angela Thirkell.

On the opposite side of the road is The Elms, Kipling's home between 1897 and 1902. Today it is a private house not open to the public. It is, however, surrounded by the magnificent Kipling Gardens. These were originally part of the village green before being incorporated into The Elms garden.

Entrance to Kipling Gardens

In the latter part of the twentieth century they had become very overgrown and plans were drawn up to use the land for housing, much to the concern of Rottingdean residents.

All was resolved. A Preservation Society bought the land and transformed it into a replica Victorian walled garden. The nearly two acres are not to be missed and are open for all to enjoy seven days a week. In 2006 the Kipling Gardens deservedly gained a Green Flag award.

Walk through the garden and come out opposite North End House. Sir Edward Burne-Jones originally joined together the neighbouring Prospect House and Aubrey House renaming them North End House. When Enid Bagnold and her husband lived here they added Gothic House to the property.

Today it is the latter which is confusingly called North End House, although this was never Burne-Jones's home. Blue plaques commemorate stays here by Angela Thirkell and Enid Bagnold but the house itself is private property.

Continue your walk south as The Green becomes the High Street and turn left along Steyning Road leading to the playing fields to St Aubyn's, a prestigious prep school. John Kipling (always referred to as "My Boy Jack" by his father) was a pupil here from 1907 to 1911 before going off to his public school at Wellington.

In the Grange museum there are school photos and some of his father's letters written from the new family home at Bateman's. "You behaved yourself like a man even when you felt homesickness...you did not blub and whine but carried on quietly", said the proud but perhaps rather cold father.

DAY TWO - WORTHING

Probably the most famous literary visitor to the town was **Oscar Wilde (1854-1900)**. At the height of his literary fame, he came to stay here with his wife and two sons in the summer of 1894, largely to avoid his creditors in London and while here wrote 'The Importance of Being Earnest'. The town not only provided the hero's name, Jack Worthing, but also a most significant part of the plot. On Wednesday, 11th July 1894 the Worthing Gazette reported that "a baby in a hamper had been found at King's Cross Station".

This story was almost perfect for Wilde's purpose. He changed the hamper to the black leather handbag, from which Lady Bracknell recoils in distaste, and the railway terminal became Victoria which "serves the Brighton line". Wilde wrote the play in only 21 days and declared it was "the best I have ever written".

To find the birthplace of this gem of English Literature, take the A259 west out of Brighton. On entering Worthing it becomes Brighton Road. Turn left on the eastern outskirts of the town on to The Esplanade. Behind a garage facing the sea stands a modern block of flats, Esplanade Court, built on the site of the house Wilde and his family rented. A plaque on the side of the building marks his brief stay in the town.

Return to the A259. On your right is Selden Road named for **John Selden (1584-1654)**, the famous antiquary and author whose manuscripts, including an original copy of the Magna Carta, became the nucleus of the British Museum collection. He was born in Salvington, on the northern outskirts of Worthing. Sadly, his thatched cottage burnt down in the 1950s and only the lintel with its Latin inscription now remains in Worthing museum.

Follow the A259 into the town centre where it joins the A24 and then turn right on the one way system to the A27, signposted Portsmouth. All is very clearly marked.

You are on track to find the home of one of the great original writers of the twentieth century, **Mervyn Peake (1911-1968)**, who spent much of his life at Burpham, ten miles North West of Worthing.

At Crossbush take the next right turning signposted to Warningcamp and Burpham. There is a magnificent view of Arundel Castle in front of you. It is very likely that Gormenghast Castle was inspired by these massive grey walls and turrets which Peake saw on the opposite side of the river, as he worked on his most famous novel.

Continue along the Burpham Road for about two miles to Reed Thatch, Peake's parents' home, on your left hand side. Mervyn and his wife Maeve spent their honeymoon here in 1937 and loved the area so much they decided to rent a small thatched cottage a mile away in Warningcamp.

When World War II broke out Peake hoped his growing artistic reputation would make him a war artist but it was not to be. His call-up papers came when his new born son was only two weeks old. Most unsuitably, he was to be a gunner and he and Maeve faced their first separation.

Memories of Warningcamp and Burpham remained with him in various postings and formed a backcloth to 'Titus Groan', written in small ruled exercise books and sent back to Maeve for safe keeping.

Maeve moved twice while he was away, first to the top floor of the Old School House in Upper Warningcamp and then to a cottage next door to Reed Thatch, known strangely as 94 Wepham. Army life had not suited Mervyn and eventually army doctors decided he was suffering a nervous breakdown. In September 1942 he was sent home to Burpham on indefinite sick leave and six months later was invalided out of the army. 'Titus Groan' was finished in Burpham.

By the time the novel was published in 1946 Mervyn, Maeve and their two children had left Sussex. They were unable to renew the cottage tenancy and instead took a studio in Chelsea. They were still frequent visitors to the family home of Reed Thatch and between 1954 and 1956, when he taught illustration at Brighton College of Art, Mervyn frequently stayed overnight in Burpham and after his death he was buried there. The inscription on his gravestone in the churchyard: "To live at all is miracle enough" is a fitting line from one of his poems.

Return to the A27 and then the A24 and retrace the road to Worthing. As the A24 reaches the northern outskirts of Worthing it changes its name to Broadwater Road, the name of this suburb. On the right-hand side, not far from the parish church, is Broadwater Cemetery, the final resting place of two important Nature writers.

The naturalist and mystic, **Richard Jefferies** was a frequent visitor to Sussex and spent the last five years of his life in Jefferies House, Jefferies Lane, Goring by Sea, now a private house. The American born naturalist and novelist **W.H.Hudson (1841-1922)**, perhaps best known for his 1910 'A Shepherd's Life', was buried by his own wish in the same cemetery as the man he so admired.

This admiration was so great it overcame the antipathy he felt for Worthing. "I hate the place" he wrote "and have never yet met anyone in it who has been of use to me. It is talk, talk, talk but never a gleam of an original or fresh remark or view of anything that does not come out of a book or a newspaper".

Turn immediately right at the cemetery's main entrance and walk to the far boundary fence. Turn left and Hudson's grave is against the fence under a row of pine trees. Around the grave is written: "He loved birds and green places and the wind on the heath and saw the brightness of the skirts of God".

IF YOU HAVE MORE TIME

If you have the luxury of a longer stay in the area we suggest a trip out of Brighton to the South Downs and especially to the area round Devil's Dyke to do some detective work. **Stella Gibbons (1902-1989)** had been a London journalist for ten years when, in 1932, she produced 'Cold Comfort Farm', a delicious parody of many pessimistic rural novels.

Over the years since the novel's first appearance, many novels and novelists have been suggested as the intended target in her writings but in an article for Punch magazine in 1966 the author herself finally made clear what and whom she was satirising.

"The large agonised faces in Mary Webb's book annoyed me...her characters also reminded me of certain people with whom I had grown up, who were, so to speak, permanently in the woodshed with door shut and preferring it that way. Parodies of both sets of characters began to prowl...in my mind...while Sheila Kaye-Smith's rather too meaningful Sussex suggested their background".

One suspects that the "certain people with whom I had grown up" refers to her immediate family, which seems to have been as dysfunctional as the Starkadders.

Stella Gibbon's comments do suggest Sussex is one intended target and recent literary research indicates the villages of Fulking and Poynings have been immortalised in Howling and the area round the Starkadder Farm. We suggest a day trip (perhaps when "the sukebind is in flower"). With the novel as a guide you may even discover what the "something nasty in the woodshed" actually was! The 77 bus goes there.

CAN I DO THESE TOURS WITHOUT A CAR?

Brighton and the south coast are easy to reach by train from both Victoria and London Bridge stations in London. Contact National Rail Enquiries on 08457 484950 or log on to www.nationalrail.co.uk.

Of course you may be planning to arrive in style, after all Brighton does have that wonderful Marina. Contact the Harbour master with berthing enquiries for your yacht on 01273 819919. And if your choice of transport is even more ambitious, nearby Shoreham Airport is available for private light aircraft to land. Telephone number for enquiries is 01273 296900.

Brighton city centre is actually much better tackled on foot. A car can be a nuisance and parking is a nightmare. Day Two's trip to Worthing could largely be done by bus. The 700 Coast Liner runs from Brighton. The suggested itinerary almost overlaps some of the Horsham exploration.

If you want to combine parts of the two trips think of taking the 23 bus service from Brighton via Worthing to Arundel. See www.stagecoachbus.com (or 01903 237661).

BEST TIME TO VISIT

The first three weeks in May see the annual Brighton Festival. First started in 1967, this is one of the foremost arts festivals in the country.

Go to www.brightonfestival.org for further information.

IF YOU HAVE CHILDREN

The Royal Pavilion is British heritage at its most eccentric but one of the most exotically beautiful buildings in Britain. Somehow the outside Indian architecture and the Chinese interior do fit together to create a uniquely attractive style. Young and old alike should have a great time exploring (the Great Kitchen is always a particular favourite).

Go to www.royalpavilion.org.uk or telephone 03000 290900.

Brighton Marina is a fascinating spot to see the boats, visit the many discount stores or enjoy bowling, indoor golf and a multi-screen cinema. A comprehensive update on all amenities is to be found at www.brightonmarina.co.uk.

Also popular with children is Volks Railway, a traditional train which runs along the seafront to the Marina.

All the information is at www.volkselectricrailway.co.uk and on 01273 292718.

Close to Worthing is Arundel Wetland Centre. Arundel Castle forms a stunning backdrop to this 65 acre home for rare wildfowl with boat safaris to glide you close up to the wildlife.

Go to www.org.uk/Arundel for more information.

CHICHESTER

West Sussex County Town

———❖———

CHICHESTER'S WRITERS

John Keats (1795-1821)

Sussex twice played an important part in John Keats' short life. First, he met the great love of his life, Isabella Jones, in 1817 when both were staying at an inn in the tiny village of Bo Peep outside Hastings (see the Rye and Hastings chapter for more information). He returned to the county a year later after the death of his brother Tom, in December 1818 from consumption (usually referred to as TB today). Tom was only 19 and his premature death shocked his older brother John, who little realised a similar fate awaited him three years later.

His friends did all they could to distract him, taking him to theatres, concerts and even a 34 round boxing tournament. One neighbour, Charles Dilke, arranged for the poet and his friend, Charles Brown, to stay in Chichester with his elderly parents. They arrived in Chichester on the night of January 21st.

Although Brown returned to London after a few days, Keats was to spend two weeks in the area both in Chichester and then further along the coast at Havant in Hampshire. It was to be a fruitful stay. Keats duly visited the cathedral and, even more significantly for his poetic output, a card party in the Vicars Hall, close to the cloisters, the probable setting for Madeleine's room in 'The Eve of Saint Agnes'.

The young poet seems to have been unaware of how memorable his poetry was to become and what effect this brief stay in Chichester would have on his writing. In one of his letters he wrote: "Nothing worth speaking of happened…I took down some of the thin paper and wrote on it a little poem called 'St Agnes Eve'". He promises to send it with his next letter "and if I should finish it a little thing called 'The Eve of St Mark'".

While staying in Chichester Keats and Brown went by post-chaise to Stansted Park to attend the dedication of its chapel, a magnificent example of Regency Gothic. They had not been able to obtain any tickets so had to remain in the porch, viewing the service with great difficulty. What did catch the poet's eye was the triple arched window in the nave with the arms of the Earl of Arundel whose family, the Fitzalans, probably built the earliest parts of the chapel in the 15th century.

He did not enjoy the ceremony but it almost certainly furnished him with the image of the triple arched window "diamonded with panes of quaint device" which shone on "the wintry noon of St Agnes Eve".

William Hayley (1745-1820)

Hayley today is known almost exclusively for his connection with William Blake (see that poet's entry below) but fame is a strange thing. There are very few today who have not heard of William Blake yet in his lifetime he struggled to make a decent living. Hayley, however, was immensely popular and respected. He was even offered the Poet Laureateship in 1790, which he turned down. But who has heard of him today?

His claim to fame is the estate he owned at Felpham, about 6 miles from Chichester, and his patronage of Blake. It was he who arranged for Blake to leave London for three years and stay near him in Felpham for a very productive phase of his life. Sadly, the house Hayley lived in there (known as the Turret House) was demolished in 1961. He and his wife had made their first married home at Eartham near Chichester, in what is now Great Ballard School.

William Blake (1757-1827)

William Blake was born in London and the capital city seems to have been his natural habitat. There was however, a highly significant three year Sussex interlude in Felpham, near Bognor, just six miles from Chichester. Generations of Promenaders and Womens Institute members must be particularly grateful for his Sussex stay since one of his great achievements while living here, perhaps inspired by the Sussex countryside, was his long poem 'Milton' written at Felpham, with its famous opening lines:

> "And did those feet in ancient times
> Walk upon England's mountains green?"

By 1800 the 43year old poet and engraver felt that life in the metropolis was clouding his vision. Just as he felt he needed a purer environment, the call came from William Hayley, a poet and biographer, living in Felpham. It was not Blake's poetic genius that Hayley was interested in but his engraving skills. After all, that was how Blake earned his living.

Hayley was a prolific writer, most of it now forgotten and he commissioned his protégé to illustrate several of his poems. In addition he wanted him to decorate his library, with up to eighteen portraits of poets. When he also promised commissions from some of his friends Blake felt it was an offer he could not refuse and in September 1800 he and his long suffering wife Kate moved into a vacant cottage in the village.

Blake's cottage and the plaque on its wall

At first the Blakes were idyllically happy. Blake loved the area. "Sussex is certainly a happy place and Felpham in particular is the sweetest spot on earth", he wrote to a friend and he was able to conscientiously complete his patron's to-do list as well as further his own poetry.

Sadly the idyll was short lived. Blake had misgivings. He was extremely comfortable in Felpham. Hayley was very kind, perhaps too kind and Blake started to feel suffocated. It was difficult for the visionary engraver to communicate with his 'Messengers from Heaven'.

Matters came to a head in late 1803 when there was a heated argument in the cottage garden with a trespassing soldier, whom Blake, perhaps venting some of his growing frustrations, unceremoniously turned out. The matter did not rest there. The soldier wanted revenge. Britain was engaged in a long and bitter war against Napoleon and a French invasion could be expected any day.

Possibly Blake had been unguarded in his comments. The soldier maliciously reported him to the authorities and Blake was arrested and charged with making seditious expressions in support of Napoleon. He was after all the poet who had earlier written a long poem in praise of the French Revolution. He was tried for treason (the soldier's original trespassing had long since been forgotten) in January 1804 in Chichester's Greyfriars, used as the city's Guildhall.

The Sussex Advertiser reported that he had used expressions such as: "Damn the King, damn all his subjects, damn his soldiers ... when Bonaparte comes ... I will help him". Things looked grim but his patron came to his rescue. He engaged the best lawyer he could to defend Blake and spoke passionately himself in defence of the poet's good character. Common sense did prevail and Blake was found not guilty. The whole incident greatly disturbed him and he returned to London with his family. Sweet Felpham had become a rather bitter memory.

Anthony Trollope (1815-1882)

It seems strange to discuss Trollope in connection with a recognisable county. Surely he belongs to Barsetshire? Although most of his life was spent in London and Essex, he did spend the final two years of his life in South Harting, nine miles from Chichester. His doctors had hoped that the good country air would improve his health but, sadly, this was not the case.

He missed the buzz of London social life and became quite depressed, especially at the fall in sales of his books. In 1882 he rallied and he and his wife, Rose, made two visits to Ireland. Out of these came the only book he was to write at Harting: 'The Land Leaguers'. Sadly, he was to write no more. His health further declined and he and Rose returned to London where he died, following a stroke, on the 6th of December, 1882.

H. G. Wells (1866-1946)

Sarah Wells, a strong minded woman, was determined that the youngest of her three sons would do well in life. Her plan was for Herbert George to become a successful shopkeeper. Her son found the prospect utterly unappealing. Ironically, his frequent failures in the retail world (he seemed to be following in the footsteps of his equally unsuccessful father) were to become a wonderful source of material for several of his highly successful novels.

Sarah Wells began her working life as a maid to the Featherstonehaugh family at Uppark, their magnificent mansion outside Harting, about nine miles north of Chichester.

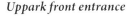

Uppark front entrance

View from rear and side

She married one of the gardeners, Joseph Wells, and her first attempt at social mobility began. She persuaded Joseph to become a shopkeeper, a job he was clearly unfitted for and over the years there was a series of failed ventures. Finally Sarah took matters into her own strong hands. She decided to leave her husband and accept an offer to return to Uppark, not this time as a lowly maid but as a very powerful Housekeeper. It was to have momentous consequences for her son.

The 14 year old Herbert had already been asked to leave his first job as a draper's assistant, an inevitable decision as more often than not he failed to turn up for work. This was followed by a failed attempt as a pupil teacher in a relative's school. So he joined his mother at Uppark, crucially being given the run of the house's vast library. He must have been like a child in a sweetshop, indiscriminately devouring every book he could lay his hands on.

His real education began here. Sarah, however, didn't see it that way. Books were all well and good for the gentry but not for people like them. They had to have a real job, preferably in a shop! She knew the area well, having been brought up in Midhurst at her parents' inn. Through contacts in the town she found him work at the chemist's shop. Shortly after this just the right job, in her eyes at least, came up and an unwilling son went to work in a draper's in Portsmouth.

Herbert hated the whole experience but stuck it out for two years, easily the longest time the youngster had kept a job. Finally he was able to persuade his mother to let him leave but only by very drastic means. He threatened suicide if she made him stay any longer. It is easy to forget how young he was, still only 17 but with a wealth of experience that would be fully exploited in his subsequent novels.

He returned to Midhurst. It was only a three hour walk away from Uppark, and became a teaching assistant, at the Grammar School where he was known.

Two years earlier the Headmaster had given him some basic Latin lessons so that he could cope with the prescriptions in the chemist's shop. The teachers at the school recognised his potential and helped him to pass his exams to become a London University science student.

Off he went to South Kensington. There was to be only one more extended visit to Uppark. He ruptured a kidney whilst playing in a football match some months after leaving university and spent the next three months convalescing there. After that he was never to live in Sussex again. But his 1909 novel 'Tono-Bungay', especially, is suffused with memories of the area around Uppark (here renamed Bladesover).

ONE DAY VISIT

Chichester, the county town, goes back to Roman times when it was known as Regnum and is remarkably easy to find one's way round, thanks to those Roman builders and the grid system they gave the town. It has a very long tradition of being the birthplace and nurturing ground of a varied collection of writers and one of today's most exciting novelists, **Kate Mosse,** author of the 2005 international best seller, 'Labyrinth', is a Chichester resident.

You don't need a car for today's city tour so unless you are staying in the centre of the city, we suggest you go straight to the Festival Theatre car park and leave your car there. The theatre opened in 1962 under the direction of Sir Laurence Olivier. Living at nearby East Dean, **Christopher Fry** maintained strong links with the theatre, where several of his plays (including a new version of Ibsen's Peer Gynt) were performed in the 1970s.

Leave the Car Park via the pedestrian underpass and turn into North Street, walking in a southerly direction. Chichester is a shopper's paradise and it may be difficult to stay focussed all day on writers. Your first port of call, however, is to feed the soul. Turn right at the Butter Market, the central crossroads.

Butter Market

The 900 year old Cathedral dominates the skyline as one drives into the city and the interior is at least as beautiful as the exterior, thanks partly to the farsighted patronage of Dean Hussey. Unlike many cathedrals, admission is free. There are also free daily guided tours.

View of the Cathedral

Hunt out the Arundel tomb in the North aisle (on your left hand side as you enter the cathedral).

It commemorates Richard Fitzalan, 13th Earl of Arundel and his Lady (the same Fitzalan family, incidentally, which built Stansted Chapel, which so inspired John Keats). These two effigies date from about 1400 and highly unusually for memorials of that date, they are holding hands. Rather touchingly, although the Earl is ramrod straight his wife is turned slightly towards him. It was this which gave **Philip Larkin** the inspiration for one of his most famous poems which is displayed beside the tomb. The old cynic comments surprisingly on the monument's meaning:

"What will survive of us is love"

There are so many other lovely things in the cathedral. While you are there make sure you find Marc Chagall's beautiful stained glass window,

Graham Sutherland's magnificent painting: 'Noli Me Tangere' and John Piper's tapestry. It is also worth noticing the marble monument to the poet **William Collins**, who died in 1759. He was born in Chichester, lived in the city most of his life and died here. Interestingly the words on the memorial are by Blake's patron, **William Hayley**.

Glance up at the cathedral spire as you come out into daylight. In his fascinating account 'A Tour through the Whole Island of Great Britain' (1724-1727) **Daniel Defoe** gives an account of his stay in Chichester, including the following legend:

> "They have a story in the city that whenever a bishop of the diocese is to die, a heron comes and sits on the pinnacle of the spire of the cathedral. This accordingly happened when Dr Williams was bishop. A butcher standing at his shop door in South Street saw it and ran in for his gun. Being a good marksman he shot the heron and killed it. His mother was very angry with him and said he had killed the bishop. The next day news came to the town that Dr. Williams was dead".

In fact the spire which interested Defoe collapsed in 1860 and the present one is Victorian.

Exit the cathedral by the main door and turn immediately left. Follow the path round to enter the cloisters. On your right is the Cloisters Café, an excellent spot for a light lunch or afternoon tea. It has a lovely garden with beautiful views of the cathedral. Continue past the café and turn left to exit into the churchyard.

The Vicars Hall is part of a row of buildings on your right-hand side. While staying in Eastgate Square, **John Keats** visited the tenant, Mrs Mary Lacy, to join her weekly card playing session. These rooms became immortalised in 'The Eve of St Agnes'. There is a pleasant café, The Buttery, in the crypt. Turn right into South Street and the Tourist Information Office is 150 metres on the right (contact them on 01243 775888 or email chitic@chichester.gov.uk).

Opposite the Vicars Hall Buttery is West Pallant. Walk down here past the redundant church, now a Red Cross centre and you will face the splendid Pallant House at the next cross roads. This early eighteenth century merchant's house has now been extended and is open as an art gallery, with an important collection including works by Graham Sutherland, Henry Moore and Paul Nash. It's well worth a visit.

Continue straight ahead into East Pallant, turning left into Baffins Lane which joins East Street. On the corner there is a large clothes shop with a colonnaded front in what was part of the former Corn Exchange. Here on Boxing Day 1896 was the first moving picture show in Chichester and one of the first cinema shows in the country. Turn right past the end of the city wall into Eastgate Square. On the far south east side of the square, at number 11, a plaque high up on the wall marks the spot where Keats stayed in January 1819.

Plaque to John Keats

Retrace your steps in East Street to the first turning on the right, Little London and continue to the T junction at the end. Turn left into Priory Road and on your right hand side you will see Priory Park with Grey Friars in the centre. The Friary existed here from 1269 and after its dissolution in 1538 the building was used as a Guildhall and the venue for the Quarter Sessions. It was here that **William Blake's** trial for sedition took place in 1804.

Turn left into Guildhall Street which joins North Street and you will see where you began this round trip and so back to the car park next to the Festival Theatre. Lunches and dinners are available at The Brasserie in the Park in the Minerva Theatre building opposite the actual Festival Theatre (reservations - 01243 782219 - often necessary during the summer Festival season).

After the morning in Chichester it's time to return to your car to drive the six miles to Felpham on the William Blake trail. Aim first for the parish church where William Hayley is buried. There is a memorial to him on the north wall of the chancel with the simple message: 'The Friend and Biographer of Cowper'.

Then drive down Limmer Lane immediately opposite to it. You will see the Thatched House pub on your right and opposite this the site of Hayley's Turret House, marked by a blue plaque. It has since been demolished to make way for modern housing. Inevitably one road bears the name Hayley Close and other houses form part of Hayley Mews.

Turn right at the Thatched House pub into Waterloo Road which becomes Blake's Road. Drive past the Fox Inn and Blake's cottage is 10 metres on your left. There is a small blue plaque on the wall dedicated to Blake the "artist, poet and mystic". Today it is surrounded by modern housing but the area still retains a very pretty village feel.

The Fox Inn (put PO22 7EH into your SatNav) has been voted South East Pub of the Year. Blake was arrested in the doorway as the soldier in question, John Scholfield, was billeted here. A blue plaque gives the details. The pub sign depicts the sailing ship, The Fox, which the artist, George Morland, painted in lieu of rent. The Fox Inn is open all day and is a good stop for refreshments on the sightseeing trail. After all this, there's a welcome breath of fresh sea air just 300 metres after Blake's cottage with a very pleasant paved walk beside the sea.

TWO DAY VISIT

Day Two is largely given over to visiting Uppark (GU31 5QR for your SatNav) in the steps of H.G.Wells. The National Trust suggests it will take you three hours and there's certainly a lot to see. It is open from Sunday to Thursday, from the end of March to the end of October. A Sunday or Wednesday afternoon in July and August would be very convenient as Stansted Park is also open on those days and times.

Leave Chichester by the A286, signposted Midhurst, and pass through Lavant. Four miles north of Chichester veer to the left onto the

B2141, signposted South Harting and Petersfield. After seven miles, turn right onto the B2146. After one mile you are in South Harting.

Anthony Trollope (1815-1882) spent the final two years of his life here at a house called The Grange, situated down North Laine close by the Ship Inn. Little remains today to show where the great novelist once lived.

Return to the B2146 (ignoring the turn to the B2141) and one and a half miles south of South Harting is the entrance to Uppark. It opens at 12.30pm and lunch in the pleasant restaurant could be an enjoyable start to your visit. Make sure you visit the Victorian kitchen and the Housekeeper's Room, where the mother of H. G. Wells reigned supreme.

Having exhausted the glories of Uppark, return to the B2146 in the direction of Compton. Carry on for another mile and take a right-hand turn into the lane at West Marden. After a mile you reach Forestside. Here turn left following signs to Stansted Park (PO9 6DX). It is open from 1.00pm to 4.00pm in the summer on Sundays and Mondays and additionally on Sunday to Wednesday afternoons in July and August. The Garden Centre and Tea Rooms are open throughout the year.

To complete this round trip, return to the lane and turn left out of Stansted Park, following signs to Aldsworth (one mile) and Funtington (three miles). Finally follow the B2178 for five miles back into Chichester.

CAN I DO THESE TOURS WITHOUT A CAR?

Chichester itself is much easier to explore on foot than by car. To visit Uppark, take the Country Liner 54 bus which operates between Chichester and Petersfield railway stations. The bus stop is about 500 metres from Uppark via a steep hill.

IF YOU HAVE CHILDREN

West Wittering Beach, an uncommercialised sandy Blue Flag beach at the entrance to Chichester Harbour is perfect for the bucket and spade brigade, or even a winter walk, although as always in this country it really needs fine weather!

Whatever the weather, The South Downs Planetarium in Chichester (www.southdowns.org.uk/sdpt or 'phone 01243 774400) can show you the stars at any time and in comfort.

To really work off some of that energy, try Harbour Park in Littlehampton, just next door to Felpham on the William Blake Trail. Here you'll find Rides and Attractions (information at www.harbourpark.com and telephone 01903 721200).

BEST TIME TO VISIT

Chichester Festival Theatre's summer season runs from mid April to the end of September (details from 01243 781312 and box.office@cft.org.uk). Within this period the annual Chichester Festivities at the end of June and the beginning of July showcase musicians and artists of national and international repute (info@chifest.org.uk).

EASTBOURNE

The Jewel of the Sussex Coast

—————

EASTBOURNE'S WRITERS

Charles Lamb (1775-1834)

One of the earliest visitors to Eastbourne was Charles Lamb. He devoted a good deal of his life to caring for his sister Mary, who had stabbed their mother to death in a fit of insanity. In spite of this trauma they were able to collaborate successfully to produce 'Lambs Tales from Shakespeare'.

Charles visited Eastbourne in the early years of the nineteenth century when it was little more than a collection of farms and scattered hamlets. He was not impressed and wrote that life had been "Dull at Worthing, Duller at Brighton but Dullest at Eastbourne".

Lewis Carroll (1832–1898)

Probably very few people today would recognise Charles Ludwidge Dodgson as the creator of Alice in Wonderland. Lewis Carroll is one of two Eastbourne residents who is much better known by his nom de plume, rather than by his given name (the other writer was George Orwell, of whom more below).

The Oxford University lecturer in mathematics had already become famous as the author of the two Alice books when he began spending his vacations here in1877. He was to return every summer for the next ten years spending a good deal of time on the beach taking photographs (a recent invention). Of the many books he wrote at this time, at least one, 'Sylvie and Bruno', was written, or at least completed, in Eastbourne.

ST CYPRIAN'S AND OTHER SCHOOLS

In the late nineteenth and early twentieth centuries the town became very popular as its many prep schools (most long since gone, leaving just two excellent ones in their place today) were filled by parents seeking a healthy environment for their sons to grow up in. One of the earliest visitors was **Beatrix Potter (1866-1943)**.

She visited the town in 1884 and 1885, "partly for Papa's health and partly for sending Bertram back to school". Her brother attended Grange School, presumably in Grange Road, although there is no trace of it now.

The family's visits to Eastbourne included trips to Pevensey Castle and Beachy Head, where they saw a wreck. There is no evidence to show how Master Potter felt about his schooldays but a beautiful environment and healthy air were, sadly, poor compensation for the many unhappy children who used to suffer under harsh regimes.

E.M.Forster (1879-1970)

At the end of the nineteenth century he was a pupil at Kent House School in Staveley Road. It was a very small establishment, with only about thirty boys. Forster thought Eastbourne was "a lovely place", but he was homesick and very unhappy at the school. He told his mother in a letter home: "you have nothing and nobody to love". More than 100 years later one can so easily picture that sad little boy.

The best known of all these former Eastbourne prep schools was St. Cyprian's, where the naturalist and writer **Gavin Maxwell (1914-1969)**, best known for his work on otters and especially for 'Ring of Bright Water', was a pupil in the 1920s.

Ten years earlier was a golden period in the history of the school, when at the same time between 1911 and 1916 **Cyril Connolly (1903-**

1976), **Cecil Beaton (1904-1980)** and **George Orwell (1903-1950)** (the last one under his real name of Eric Blair), were all contemporaries.

Connolly wrote about his unhappy school days (renaming the school St. Wulfrics) in 'Enemies of Promise' but for real bile one has to turn to Orwell's account in 'Such, Such were the Days'. Strikingly, one of his abiding memories of the school is the guilt and bewilderment he frequently felt at accusations of committing nameless crimes against the school's rigid rules. It is easy to speculate that the seeds for '1984' were sown here.

Even more interesting, the pretty village of Willingdon, a mere three miles away, was a popular destination for half-holiday walks from the school.

Connolly wrote: "We often walked together over the Downs in our green jerseys and our corduroy breeches discussing literature". The farm in 'Animal Farm' is also situated in Willingdon, which also has a Red Lion pub.

Chalk Farm   *Red Lion pub*

T S Eliot (1888-1965)

In 1915 T S Eliot and his first wife, Vivien Haigh-Wood, spent their honeymoon in Eastbourne. Was it a happy time? Who can tell? Certainly Vivien liked the town and visited it regularly but it was an unhappy marriage and one suspects Eliot did not look back on his time here with warm affection.

He joined the publishing house of Faber and Faber as an editor in 1925 and subsequently spent all his working life there. He was responsible for many of the twentieth century's most famous writers being published by the firm but he failed to recognise the greatness of 'Animal Farm', rejecting it for being politically out of touch. It is an interesting coincidence that its author was a prep school boy in Eastbourne when his potential publisher was on honeymoon there. Is it too far fetched to speculate that the novel's setting in Willingdon subliminally reminded Eliot of the start of a very unhappy period in his life?

Thomas Huxley (1825-1895)

This eminent biologist, one time president of the Royal Society and strong campaigner for the theory of evolution, gloried in his nickname of 'Darwin's Bulldog'. It was Huxley's extensive writing which really popularised Darwin's work.

Never one to suffer fools gladly; he revelled in anti-religious controversy, loving to engage in intellectual battles (notably with Liberal Prime Minister William Ewart Gladstone).

His recurring depression would then disappear to be replaced by furious bad temper at his misguided opponents. In 1890 at the height of his fame he and his wife Henrietta came to live in a house specially built for them and called Hodeslea, the Anglo Saxon version of Huxley, or so he alleged.

Eastbourne was just the tonic he needed. He was 65, his health was not good and there were concerns about his heart. In the time he had left from campaigning, lecturing and writing scientific papers he cultivated his garden assiduously and walked every day across the Downs to Beachy Head. Although his health did show some improvement, he was in no fit state to cope with a virulent outbreak of influenza which swept across the whole of Eastbourne and his death occurred five years after his arrival in the town

Noel Streatfield (1895-1986)

A very different author was born in the year of Huxley's death. Noel Streatfield moved here from St Leonard's in 1911 when her clergyman father, William Champion Streatfield, was appointed vicar of St Mary's church in Old Town.

St.Mary's church

The family remained here until 1928, when he was appointed Bishop of Lewes. The ups and downs of her upbringing were recounted in 'A Vicarage Family', written in 1963 when she was 68.

After leaving Eastbourne School of Domestic Economy, on the outbreak of the First World War, she worked in a military kitchen at the same time writing and producing children's plays at Eastbourne's Winter Gardens.

Theatre was her first love. Having trained at RADA, she successfully toured South Africa, New Zealand and Australia but her final career decision was made on the sudden death of her father in 1929.

She returned home and wrote her first novel: 'The Whicharts' which received high praise from John Galsworthy. There was no stopping her writing now and, drawing heavily on her stage experience, she produced in all 64 books, of which 49 were for children.

Her 1936 best-seller 'Ballet Shoes' is probably the best known, with its realistic portrayal of the hard work, sweat and tears which lie behind the glamour of stage performances.

Rumer Godden (1907-1998)

Although born in Eastbourne, Rumer Godden spent her early childhood commuting between Bengal in Asia and Moira House Girls School in her birthplace. In adult life she went on to produce over seventy works including 24 novels, collections of poetry and children's books.

Her first great success was 'Black Narcissus', published in 1939 and never since out of print. She often returned to Sussex, spending several happy years in Rye. Have a look at the Rye and Hastings chapter for a more detailed account of her life.

ONE DAY VISIT

Seafront with pier

Eastbourne is a delightful town and a drive along its seafront is in someway a nostalgic journey to a gentler, more elegant age. In the middle of the nineteenth century most of Eastbourne belonged to either the Duke of Devonshire or, to a much lesser extent, Carew Davies Gilbert. These two landowners saw the town's potential and employed the best architects available.

As a consequence of their far sighted planning and extensive building work in the 1870s 'The Empress of Watering Places', as it became known, developed with its wide, tree lined streets and elegant squares. In addition, the town's beautiful position at the foot of the Downs, sheltered by Beachy Head, produces its own micro climate. It has been a popular destination for visitors, many of them with literary connections, for well over a hundred and fifty years.

A visit to the Tourist Information Centre in Cornfield Road (0871 663 0031), makes a good first port of call or visit the website at <u>www. visiteastbourne.com</u>.

On leaving the Tourist Office, turn immediately right into Hyde Gardens. **Angela Carter (1940-1992)**, the daughter of a journalist, was born here at number 12, although she left Eastbourne at a young age and grew up in London and the North of England.

She evokes a carefree childhood in one essay, describing how "life passed at a languorous pace, everything was gently untidy and none of the clocks told the right time". She is best known for her modern fairy tales filled with symbolism and fantasy.

A very near neighbour, **Lewis Caroll,** was interested in similar topics a hundred years earlier. The next turning on the right (after the Tourist Information Office) brings you to Lushington Road. Number 7, now a dental practice, but formerly Mrs Grundy's guest house, was where he spent his summer holidays between 1877 and 1887 A blue plaque 'to perpetuate his memory with gratitude' was placed here in 1954 by the Eastbourne Civic Society.

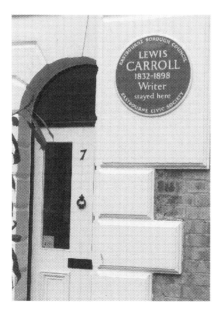

Lewis Caroll plaque

From Lushington Road go back to Cornfield Road and turn right and travel a short distance to the roundabout with its war memorial cross. Go round this and take the last exit into South Street (one way). Keep to the left and at the end bear left into College Road.

Edna Lyall (1857 -1903) lived here at number 6 (now a medical practice), from 1884 until her death in 1903. Her real name was actually Ada Ellen Bayley, nine letters of which formed the anagram of her pen name. She had family connections here, as her brother-in-law was curate of nearby St Saviour's Church and also first vicar of St. Peter's (this church has since disappeared).

She herself presented the church with a peal of three bells named after the leading characters in three of her novels: Donovan, Erica and Hugo.

This radical novelist championed Irish Home Rule, a highly contentious issue, in earlier novels and then turned her attention to criticism of the Boer War in the two novels produced in her Eastbourne years: 'Doreen' (1889) and 'The Hinderers' (1902).

Return to South Street, turn right and take the second left (first is no entry) round a small island, approaching traffic lights. Go through these onto Gildredge Road and take the second right down Lushington Road again. At its end turn right and at the roundabout take the second exit into Trinity Trees.

Hartington Place is first on your right. It was here at number 8 Hartington Mansions that **T.S.Eliot** and his wife Vivien spent their honeymoon in 1915.

Continue to the end of Hartington Place as it meets Grand Parade just to the east of the bandstand. Turn right and Burlington Place is the second turning on the right. **Gilbert Foyle (1886-1971)**, the founder of Foyle's Bookshop in London, lived here at 4 Ashburnham Court. There are more recent buildings on the site today.

Foyle is remembered in the town with great affection for his wonderful generosity, giving the money which enabled Eastbourne Council to buy the South Downs area around Beachy Head. The Wish Tower Café was also built at his expense.

There is one more site to track down in this area. Retrace your steps to Grand Parade, turn left and Cavendish Place is the fifth turning on the left, easy to pick out opposite the delightful Victorian pier. There is still a hotel on the corner and here at number 4 was **Friedrich Engels'** holiday home on his regular visits to England. Maybe when **Karl Marx** and his family came to visit him from June to July 1881 they also stayed here as Engels' guests.

The twin founders of communism had worked together on 'The Communist Manifesto' of 1848. Engels was a great financial supporter of Marx, who was frequently reduced to great poverty and possibly the main purpose of this visit, only two years before his death, was to improve Marx's health.

There was another important writer here at the same time. Perhaps The Communist Manifesto's authors stopped to pass the time of day with Alice in Wonderland's originator on one of his annual visits. Eastbourne was quite small then and surely their paths must have crossed. One wonders which 'wonderland' was the more unlikely.

After this morning's intensive sightseeing you need a break for lunch and there are plenty of reasonably priced eateries in the town. The morning's expedition could easily be accomplished on foot, but you may prefer to use a car this afternoon.

To start the afternoon's exploration, drive out of Eastbourne town centre along Upperton Road bearing left into The Goffs. This becomes High Street then Church Street. Turn left into Vicarage Road and on the corner of Vicarage Drive (second right) is the pretty pink washed early home of **Noel Streatfield**.

Go along Vicarage Drive and turn into Summerdown Road. Number 67 was the site of **St. Cyprian's School.**

The school was burnt down in May 1939 but St Cyprian's Lodge stands at the old entrance gate. A plaque marks the spot of such a significant seat of learning. It is possible to pursue your research into the school further and Eastbourne Library (in the town centre at the bottom of Grove Road) has an archive about it. There are some fascinating documents which indicate the future paths some of the boys would take.

At the end of the Winter Term in 1916 Eric Blair (later George Orwell) won the Classics prize, Cyril Connolly won the English prize and Cecil Beaton the Drawing prize. The library also has a copy of the school magazine, St Cyprian's Chronicle for Christmas 1916, which shows that at the same time these potentially famous Old Boys were studying hard they were also performing in a 'Dramatic Entertainment'.

Orwell acted the part of Mr.Wardle in 'Mr. Jingle's Wooing', based on excerpts from 'Pickwick Papers' and was described as "exceedingly good in a difficult part". Connolly meanwhile, bravely played Miss Wardle, which "showed him to be an artist of exceptional merit". However Orwell later remembered the school, life there was clearly not all bad.

How different schools are today! Nearby is the leading girls' public school, Moira House, where Rumer Godden and later Prunella Scales were educated. Carry on south on Summerdown Road and turn left onto Paradise Drive (well named for its views across the golf course and the sea). Turn right into Link Road and then right again into Carlisle Road. The school buildings are on the left.

Continue your literary exploration of this pretty Meads village area of Eastbourne by turning left where Carlisle Road meets Meads Road and then right into St John's Road. Cyril Connolly, after a distinguished career as an author and journalist, including founding and editing 'Horizon', returned to Eastbourne in 1970 to live at 48 St John's Road, where he died six years later.

Turn into Buxton Road and on the corner of this and Staveley Road is Hodeslea, Thomas Huxley's home for the last five years of his life. There is a commemorative plaque on the wall and although the house is privately owned, Huxley's domed library with its stained glass window is visible from the outside. He had written to a friend: "With three coats on I find the air on Beachy Head eminently refreshing". As you will see later on this literary tour, a few minutes brisk walking will quickly take you from Huxley's house to the dramatic headland.

Round the corner from Hodeslea, in Staveley Road, is where E.M.Forster spent his prep school years at Kent House School, a tiny school with just thirty pupils. And so as Huxley was moving in to Eastbourne in 1890, the young Forster was getting ready to move out for his Public School education in Kent at Tonbridge School. Sadly, Kent House is yet another of the Eastbourne Prep Schools which has gone.

Make your way down Buxton Road to Chesterfield Road and head north to the intersection with Milnthorpe Road. Rumer Godden was born here at number 30.

From here it's less than a five minute car drive to Beachy Head.

For your younger back seat passengers this sight might suddenly be of interest. This is the inspiration for **David** and **Ronda Armitage's** bestselling children's series: 'The Lighthouse Keeper'.

The Old Beachy Head Lighthouse

But this dramatically beautiful promontory has a much more melancholy reputation too, from the many suicides it has witnessed and, sadly, still does. Help is always at hand from the phone box at the cliff edge, with the Samaritans' telephone number clearly displayed.

One of the earliest recorded visitors to the headland was **Edward Lear (1812-1888)**, who came here in 1862, staying at the Sussex Hotel while he worked on sketches for a painting of Beachy Head, commissioned by Henry Grenfell, the MP for Stoke-on-Trent.

The Victorian poet, **Algernon Swinburne**, had great affection for Eastbourne and especially for Beachy Head, visiting it several times. Writing to a friend in November 1886, he said "Come and see me if you can on Friday next and I will read you a lyric made near Beachy Head while returning from a long walk thither. I am very much in love with Eastbourne. Do you know it?".

One distinguished visitor is still here. After his death in 1895, in accordance with his last request, **Friedrich Engels'** ashes were scattered in the sea off Beachy Head.

H.G.Wells often holidayed here, first in 1893. He stayed at 6 New Cottages, Beachy Head Road and on a later visit had his first flight in one of the sea planes which operated from the beach. Literary holiday makers continued into the twentieth century.

The poet **Rupert Brooke** made several visits, partly because his uncle, the Revd. Charles Clement Cotterill, had retired to Eastbourne and was living in the Meads area. Brooke himself stayed in the Beachy Head Hotel in 1911 to complete his dissertation. This hotel has since been destroyed by fire.

It's time now to leave this awe inspiring lonely spot. A left hand turn from the Beachy Head road will take you to the A259 and a five minute drive to Friston Church and village pond.

Friston Pond

It is an idyllic beauty spot and was home to the popular children's author **E. E. Nesbit (1858-1924)**. She had already written her most famous novel: 'The Railway Children' in 1906 before renting Crowlink House from 1911 to 1915. Here she certainly wrote one book, 'The Incredible Honeymoon'.

A left turn from the pond quickly brings you to her home, now private property. The road itself is a dead end, leading to beautiful Downland walks but there is a chance to turn your car round in the National Trust car park. Even better would be to park and stretch your legs amid this beautiful scenery.

And now you can retrace your route and return to Eastbourne. There is no better antidote to the serious and sometimes gloomy thoughts which Beachy Head brings, than to mentally replace them with the delightful illustrations of plump rosy-cheeked toddlers produced by writer and artist **Mabel Lucie Attwell (1878-1964)**. She and her husband lived in a variety of Sussex homes including Mermaid Street, Rye and Church House, Litlington before moving to Ocklynge Manor in Mill Road.

Ocklynge Manor, Mill Road with a plaque to Mabel Lucy Attwell

Turn right on the A259 and follow this road as it becomes Church Street, High Street then The Goffs. Turn left onto Upperton Road, which becomes Willingdon Road.

Ocklynge Avenue is the fifth turning on the right, with Mill Road the first turning again on the right. There is a plaque here recording Mabel Lucie Attwell's time in Eastbourne. Sadly her son died here in 1939, followed two years later by her husband. They were both buried in East Dean churchyard and Mabel Lucie Attwell herself moved away first to London and then to Cornwall.

TWO DAY VISIT

Today's exploration takes us outside Eastbourne into beautiful Downland countryside.

From the town centre, take Upperton Road, which as it goes north turns into Willingdon Road and then the A2270, signposted London. First stop is Willingdon village, three miles from the town centre. Although George Orwell never identified the location of Animal Farm, many locals are convinced that it is based on Chalk Farm in Willingdon. George Orwell and fellow St Cyprian schoolboys would walk the two hour round trip on half holidays and the village location for the farm in 'Animal Farm' is in Willingdon.

Interestingly, one Saturday in the novel, Mr Jones, the cruel farmer, goes into the village "and got so drunk at the Red Lion that he did not come back to the farm until midday on Sunday". The Red Lion is still operating in the village today. Orwell himself made no further comment and you need to draw your own conclusions.

Treat yourself to coffee or tea in the Secret Garden at Chalk Farm Hotel and Garden Centre and take a peep at the Orwell Lounge, now licensed for Civil Weddings. Certainly you may be walking through the original Animal Farm (for more detailed information click on www. chalkfarm.org).

Rejoin the A2270 and at the Polegate crossroads go straight ahead. On your right hand side is Wooton Manor. This 17th century manor house was the early home of **Elizabeth David (1913-1992)**, one of the most significant writers of the twentieth century. In a few short years she revolutionised the British public's eating habits.

Daughter of Rupert Gwynne, Conservative M.P. for Eastbourne, she was sent to the Sorbonne in1932 aged 19 to learn French and her love for French food began.

Her subsequent life reads like a racy novel with adventurous, frequently dangerous, travels with a series of lovers across Europe. Reaching Cairo during the Second World War she started work for the

Ministry of Information and met and married Lieutenant–Colonel Tony David. The marriage failed but she retained her husband's surname.

Returning to England in 1946, she was shocked by the blandness of British food and in 1950 published 'Mediterranean Food', to be quickly followed by many other influential cookery books. At that time, even olive oil was virtually unknown as a cooking aid and was much more commonly used to cure earache. Her amazed readers were introduced to such exotic fare as pasta, courgettes and aubergines. Today it is so difficult to imagine the dull diet she reacted against.

Turn left down the simply named The Street and you will reach the small hamlet of Lullington. This village and the surrounding area figures in a somewhat unlikely Sussex writer's work. The immensely successful actor **Dirk Bogarde** (Derek van den Boogaerde), the son of Ulric and Margaret, was born in Hampstead of mixed Belgian and Scottish ancestry but spent most of his early life here with his older sister Elizabeth and their adored nanny, Lally.

He wrote about it in his 1977 first volume of memoirs 'A Postillion Struck by Lightning' and in two novels 'Great Meadow' (1992) and 'Closing Ranks' (1997). More than anything, these writings reveal a great love for the natural world of this part of Sussex.

Much of Lullington village is outwardly similar to that described by Bogarde. On the Downs the magnificent prehistoric chalk carving of the Long Man of Wilmington is clearly visible.

Have a look as well at the tiny village church. It is only about sixteen feet square and seats twenty, all that remains of the original thirteenth century church, largely destroyed under Oliver Cromwell.

And now you have a choice of direction. Eastbourne lies well positioned between Lewes and Hastings. From Lullington return to the A27 and travel the 7 miles to Lewes. On the way there you can easily pick up the Bloomsbury Trail (much more detail about this will be found in the Lewes section).

Alternatively, return to the crossroads at Polegate and turn left following directions along the A22 then the A27 to Hastings. It's about 20 miles (consult the Rye and Hastings chapter for more information). You are also very close to Drusillas, the zoo and adventure playground described in the Lewes chapter.

CAN I DO THESE TOURS WITHOUT A CAR?

The centre of Eastbourne is easily explored on foot, although a walk out to Beachy Head would be more challenging on two legs, as would Day Two's itinerary. There is a half hourly bus services (Route 12A) daily from Eastbourne to Brighton via Beachy Head (full details at www. buses.co.uk).

In fact look out for these buses even if you do have your own transport. They sport appropriate and delicious puns on their sides: Cliff Hanger, Up the Downs, and Sea Front and Back are some of our favourites.

To retrace George Orwell's boyhood walks from St Cyprian's to Willingdon you'll need to arm yourself with Ordnance Survey Map 123 (Eastbourne and Beachey Head). To get to Eastbourne in the first place by public transport is simple on a day trip from London. Train journeys from London Victoria take approximately 90 minutes.

BEST TIME TO VISIT

Twice a year Eastbourne puts on its best dress and shows off to the outside world. The third week in June sees the world class International Tennis Tournament on the grass courts at Devonshire Park. This is a very popular pre-Wimbledon event. You may even see some of the stars in town (www.LTA.org.uk).

In the third week of August, look up to the skies for four days during the international Airbourne Festival. This is the biggest air show in the south and free to watch from most of the sea front, on the beach and the Downs. Overseas military aircraft and the RAF, including The Red Arrows formation flying display, are all there (www.eastbourneairshow. com).

IF YOU HAVE CHILDREN

In the season, between April and October, the delightful Dotto mini train operates a regular service along the seafront. It would be a fun way of approaching some literary sites as well as the children's play areas of

Treasure Island, Fort Fun and, of course, the pier. (www.stagecoachbus. com/eastsussex or 08456 002299)

At East Dean is the Seven Sisters Sheep Centre – a working farm with a very large collection of sheep breeds. With lambing in the spring, shearing and sheep milking in the summer and tractor rides through out the year, it is an ideal attraction for families.

Visit   www.sheepcentre.co.uk   (01323   423302)   for   more information.

At Beachy Head is the Countryside Centre's unique blend of information and entertainment relating to the locality (www.beachyhead. org or 01323 737273).

You are very close to the excellent small zoo and adventure playground of Drusillas on the Day 2 itinerary (www.drusillas.co.uk or 01323 874100)

And for a fresh view of this seaside town, why not do just that and see it from the sea.

Sussex Voyages (www.sussexvoyages.co.uk or 0845 8387114) offer a thrilling way to explore the area's coastal heritage on board their purpose built Rigid Hulled Inflatable Boat (RHIB) All the voyages are professionally guided.

HORSHAM

A Fountain, a Mill and a Hospital: Time Well Spent

The historic town of Horsham takes its name from an Anglo Saxon word meaning "horse pasture". Boasting a fascinating memorial fountain to the poet Shelley, the oldest smock windmill in the country two miles away, where Hilaire Belloc lived for many years and the famous Christ's Hospital School, it certainly deserves its town motto: 'Time Well Spent'.

HORSHAM'S WRITERS

Percy Bysshe Shelley (1792-1822)

Shelley was born and raised at Field Place, in Warnham, two miles NW of Horsham, the eldest son of a highly conservative squire who was heir to a baronetcy. The poet's unusual middle name came from his rather worldly American grandfather, who intended his grandson as his ultimate heir. He viewed his young grandson's unconventional views with amused indulgence. He may even have seen something of himself in him. After all, grandfather Bysshe had eloped with his first wife and history repeated itself with his grandson, though the older man had the good sense to marry wealthy heiresses who, in both cases, predeceased him. All young Shelley gained from his elopements was public condemnation.

When the nineteen year old Shelley was expelled from Oxford University for publishing a pamphlet entitled: 'The Necessity of Atheism', his grandfather's affectionate tolerance for his radical views ceased. The rift with his family became permanent when, later the same year, he eloped to Scotland with 16 year old Harriet Westbrook.

Her father owned a London coffee house and she was clearly not the sort of wife a baronet's heir was expected to marry. Shelley was disinherited and became completely estranged from his family. Now he was left largely penniless. The young couple quickly became estranged and five years after the unhappy Harriet's suicide, Shelley was free to marry his second wife, Mary, the author of 'Frankenstein'.

It was an interesting choice to commemorate the town's most famous son (albeit one who spent only the first ten years of his life there before boarding school and later family estrangement intervened) with a fountain and a controversial design at that. One suspects that Shelley would have been delighted that he was still causing controversy nearly 200 years after his death! His first wife drowned herself in 1816 when she was still only 21 and, 6 years later when he was not yet 30, Shelley also died by drowning in a boating accident off the coast of Italy at La Spezia.

Alfred Lord Tennyson (1809-1892)

He is usually thought of in connection with his Lincolnshire birthplace, or his later beloved Isle of Wight.

Tennyson can also be claimed for its own by Sussex – but only just. He needed somewhere sufficiently off the beaten track to escape his adoring readers, who found it far too easy to stalk the Grand Old Man of Letters in Farringford on the Isle of Wight. Aldworth, his new home on the slopes of Blackdown Hill, is actually on the Sussex/Surrey border but is certainly on the Sussex side and little more than a 20 mile drive from Horsham.

The house was built to the Tennysons' design in 1868 and given the name of his wife's family home in Berkshire. He describes how she too came to share his joy in the surrounding countryside:

"You came and looked and loved the view
Long known and loved by me
Green Sussex fading into blue
With one grey glimpse of sea"

The poet spent every summer at Aldworth until his death here in 1892. He was at his happiest walking along the crest of the Down, what is now called Tennyson's Lane and this was where he produced much of his greatest poetry, including many of the Arthurian poems.

Francis Thompson (1859-1907)

If ever a poet conformed to the stereotype of a typical poet that one was Francis Thompson with his unhappy tormented life. He was born in Lancashire, the son of a doctor and was expected to follow in his father's footsteps. His medical studies however ended disastrously.

He failed his final examinations three times and left Medical School with a first hand knowledge of drugs - illegal ones - but little of practical value. At twenty six he left home for London, working first as a bookseller's messenger. He quickly lost this position as his drug habit became more and more demanding.

Sleeping on the Thames Embankment and under the arches at Charing Cross he became more and more destitute, with any money he could beg or borrow going on laudanum, a form of opium and his drug of choice. But throughout all this degradation he never stopped writing poetry.

When he sent examples of his work to 'Merry England', a Catholic journal, its editor Wilfrid Meynell realised at once he was dealing with a genius. It must have taken some insight to see past the figure Thompson presented: "He was in rags, without stockings, his coat torn and no shirt. He seemed in the last stage of physical collapse", said the editor of that first meeting.

Meynell set himself the Herculean task of rehabilitating his new found protégé, first persuading him to stay at the White Canons monastery in Storrington, near his own country house at Amberley. The year spent there was hailed as a great success and Thompson returned to London to lodge near the Meynells' London home in Bayswater. The poetry writing continued at a furious pace and his best known piece: "The Hound of Heaven", was written at this time.

The recovering opium addict quickly slipped back to his old ways. Meynell's next solution was to get him away from the stresses of life in London to the peaceful environment of the Franciscan friars of Crawley Down. History repeated itself and they had no more long term success than the Storrington monks had before them.

He did write to Meynell in appreciation of religious hospitality: "I get better food than I ever had in lodgings since Storrington". A return to London undid all their good work.

Ever solicitous Meynell had one final solution and arranged for Thompson to stay with his friend Wilfrid Blunt at Newbuildings Place in Southwater outside Horsham. Thompson spent the summer of 1907 there still taking his regular doses of laudanum. In the October he returned to London even weaker than when he left and the following month died of tuberculosis.

Hilaire Belloc (1870-1953)

More than most, James Hillarie Pierre Belloc could be called the unofficial Sussex Poet Laureate, although he was actually born in France during a violent thunderstorm (hence his mother's nickname for him of 'Thunderer', highly appropriate for one having his sometimes violent temper). The family made a dramatic escape to England on the outbreak of the Franco Prussian War when he was only three days old. His French lawyer father had poor health and died aged 42 when his son was only two years old, so his English mother was left with the task of raising her two children on her own. She moved to Slindon and Hilaire Belloc's lifelong love affair with Sussex began.

In 1905, now a highly successful writer, he left his London home and returned with his wife Elodie and five children to Courthill Farm in Slindon. But eighteen months later it was time for another move, this time to Shipley, six miles south of Horsham. This was his home until he died, although he seems to have spent more time away travelling than actually in residence. Nevertheless his heart belonged to Sussex:

> "I never get between the pines
> But I smell the Sussex air;

Nor I never come on a belt of sand
But my home is there"

Belloc's Windmill

There must have been something in the genes. Belloc's sister, Marie Adelaide, became **Mrs Belloc Lowndes** and under this name was a successful writer of detective stories. The most successful was 'The Lodger' (1913), which was an imaginative reconstruction of the Jack the Ripper murders. The novel has been filmed three times, most recently in 1944.

Georgette Heyer (1902-1974)

It seems unlikely that this doyen of historical romances ran a sports shop with her husband in Horsham for several years. Unlikely, but absolutely true!

Some of her early married life, however, was spent in much more distant parts. Her mining engineer husband, Ronald Rougier, had postings both in Tanganyika (Tanzania today) and Macedonia. In the former they lived in an elephant grass hut deep in the African bush. Heyer was the first white woman her servants had ever seen.

In Macedonia she nearly died after a badly administered anaesthetic. It was this which finally made them both realise they needed a much more settled life if they were to bring up a family successfully. Rougier gave up his job and they returned to England in 1929 where Heyer, by now a successful writer (even while in Tanganyika with little access to the reference books about Regency England, the subject of her writing), became the main bread winner.

Rougier's first attempt at a radical career change was to adapt some of his mining expertise into running a gas and coke company. This enterprise failed and after they had moved to Sussex he borrowed money from Heyer's aunts to buy a Horsham sports shop. In 1932 her only child, Richard, was born whom she described as: "my most notable (indeed peerless) work". It is a touchingly honest comment from one who abhorred publicity. She refused to give interviews, much to her publisher's dismay. When Richard was two years old the couple moved to Slinfold, a small community west of Horsham. It was an easy 3 mile commute from here to the town centre to run the business. Heyer's younger brother, Boris, lived above the shop and helped Rougier while she concentrated on her writing.

Ronald, however, was still restless. He had always cherished a dream of becoming a barrister and it was while they lived in Slinfold that his wife made possible this final career change. She was able to support her small family by her increasingly successful novel writing and amongst others produced her most famous historical novel, 'Regency Buck' in 1935.

The family moved from the Horsham area in 1939 when her husband finally qualified, going first to Brighton and then to London. At last, after several false starts, he had found his niche and went on to become an eminent lawyer. Meanwhile, Georgette Heyer herself, almost single handed, established the historical romance genre.

OTHER WRITERS

Poets of Christ's Hospital

Is there something in the air in this part of Sussex? Almost all the significant writers in the area seem to have been poets. Perhaps it's the beauty of the landscape which develops the lyrical sense. In 1902 Christ's Hospital School moved to Horsham from the City of London where it had been founded by Edward VI in 1552 as a charity school. The name 'Hospital' has nothing to do with medicine but refers to the monks' hospitality.

Distinguished Old Boys from that first incarnation include Charles Lamb and Samuel Taylor Coleridge. They were contemporaries and continued friends in later life. In Horsham, however, it is two war poets, one from the First World War and one from the Second, who are particularly significant.

Edmund Blunden (1896-1974)

Edmund Blunden won an entrance scholarship to the school and in 1914 the gifted schoolboy clearly had a very promising literary career in front of him. At just eighteen years old he published two collections of poetry but then a few months later the whole world changed on the outbreak of war.

He deferred his place at Oxford University, for which he had been awarded a scholarship and instead enlisted in the Royal Sussex Regiment. He was to be awarded the Military Cross for his bravery at Ypres and the Somme. Throughout the war the young officer wrote of its horrors. He picked up his academic life at Oxford University after the war, where he was to become Fellow and tutor of English at Merton College, combining this with his highly regarded poetic output.

Keith Douglas (1920-1944)

He showed similar early promise. He came to the school as an eleven year old in 1931 and when still only 16 had one of his poems published in 'New Verse'. By an interesting coincidence, in 1938 he became an undergraduate at Merton College Oxford where his tutor was Edmund Blunden. The older poet immediately recognised the younger one's potential. To some extent history repeated itself for this Christ's Hospital Old Boy. He too enlisted when war broke out and was commissioned in 1941. He too gave vent to much of his feeling about the war in magnificent poetry. There the similarity sadly ends. Douglas took part in the Normandy D Day landings but was killed three days later. He had already been recognised as a significant poet.

Wilfrid Meynell (1852-1948)

Today Meynell's reputation comes almost exclusively from his patronage of many writers whom he befriended when they came to his notice as editor of the Catholic periodical 'Merry England'.

Although their main home was in London, in Bayswater, Wilfrid and Alice Meynell also bought Humphrey's Homestead in Greatham, twenty miles from Horsham. This consisted of an eighty acre estate with six houses on it. Many of the important literary figures of the early twentieth century found solace there from the hurly burly of London life. Sadly, one guest, D.H. Lawrence, rather abused their hospitality. After living with the family for six months in 1915, he wrote 'England my England', an unkind story based on the family.

Alice Meynell (1847-1922)

Was Alice Meynell the original Superwoman?! A distinguished poet, essayist and suffragette (not to mention mother to nine children), she was actually better known to the reading public in her lifetime than her husband, whom she married in 1877. Both she and her husband published a phenomenal amount and supported their large family solely through their literary earnings. No less a writer than Thomas Hardy thought she should be appointed Poet Laureate in 1913 on the death of Alfred Austin (who? you may well ask – his poetic reputation has not lived on). Robert Bridges was appointed instead and the literary world has had to wait almost one hundred years for the first woman to occupy the position.

Wilfrid Blunt (1840-1922)

Wilfrid Scawen Blunt poet, diplomat and traveller spent the last 27 years of his life in Southwater, three miles south of Horsham, as a country squire.

This larger than life character with his exotic lifestyle must have caused quite some comment on his estate. The second son of a wealthy squire who owned 4,000 acres in north Sussex, which he himself inherited in 1867 when his older brother died, his own connections with this part of the county go right back to his birth at Petworth House where his aunt, later Lady Leconfield, was living. As an adult he became a diplomat and it was at this time that he wrote many of the poems which appeared in his 'Collected Poems' published towards the end of his life in 1914.

He married Lady Annabel Noel, Lord Byron's granddaughter and after an inheritance enabled him to leave the Diplomatic Corps, the couple travelled widely together especially in Arabia and India. They shared a passion for Arab horses and were largely responsible, through the Crabbet Arabian Stud, in eradicating breeding defects in these horses. In Turkey they wore local dress, riding on horseback in harsh weather and sleeping on the ground and in Arabia Blunt converted to Islam.

Wherever he travelled he was always highly critical of British imperialism. In fact, earlier in 1887, he had been imprisoned in Galway for a passionate, if somewhat ill judged, speech in favour of Irish Home Rule. In time the couple drifted apart. His many close female friendships were not conducive to a happy married life.

He moved out of the matrimonial home of Crabbet Park, near Turners Hill, into Newbuildings Place, just south of Horsham which he had recently inherited. Here he rode round his estate in flowing Bedouin robes. 'Wilfrid of Arabia' was at least as committed to the Arab cause and way of life as the more famous Lawrence.

At the end of his life he found the winters in Sussex too cold and instead spent them more comfortably in Egypt. He returned in the summer months and entertained lavishly at Newbuildings Place.

Here fellow poets, including his near neighbour Hilaire Belloc and the dying Francis Thompson staying on his estate, were very frequent visitors. In 1914 there was the 'Peacock Dinner', given in his honour by younger poets, such as Ezra Pound and W.B.Yeats, at which a roast peacock was served.

Blunt died in 1922. On his death bed he returned to his earlier Roman Catholicism but he had failed to change his will. In this he had asked that verses from the Koran should be read over his grave when he was buried. He was interred in his Arabian travelling blanket in the woods at Newbuildings Place, with both Christian and Islamic rites. On his tomb are inscribed lines from his 1881 poem 'Chanclebury Ring'. He always stressed that this was the correct spelling of Chanctonbury Ring:

"Dear checker-work of woods, the Sussex Weald
If a name thrills me yet of things on earth
That name is thine".

ONE DAY VISIT

Horsham may have a long and venerable history but that does not prevent its being right up to date where tourism is concerned. The Horsham Town Trail is a self guided walk round the town's historic town centre with a leaflet about it available from the Tourist Information Centre. Even more user friendly is an MP3 audio trail, which can be downloaded from www.visithorsham.co.uk

Begin your literary tour in West Street at the Shelley Fountain, close by the Bus Station. The whole route is pedestrianised.

From the Piries Place car park walk all the way down East Street, go through Market Square and down Middle Street. Cross over The Causeway and go along West Street and you will see the Fountain.

Shelley's Fountain

This is less than five minutes walk from the car parks in Piries Place (and Swan Walk). Love it or loathe it, it is certainly unlikely you have seen or will see anything comparable. Designed by Angela Conner and erected in 1996, this huge water globe was inspired by Shelley's 1816 poem 'Mont Blanc'. Although its official title is 'The Rising Universe', it has been seen by some, perhaps rather unkindly, as a gigantic egg in the process of hatching. More sympathetic critics see it as a symbol of the imagination. It may not be fully in keeping with the shopping centre where it is placed but this very inelegance seems a perfect monument to Horsham's awkward son.

Continue along West Street (confusingly walking in an easterly direction) turning right into The Causeway, an ancient and tranquil area with a mixture of 15th and 16th century houses.

First stop here is Causeway House, dating from 1450, which houses the Horsham Museum and Tourist Office.

Horsham Museum

The museum is a delightful pot-pourri of exhibits with a whole room on the first floor devoted to Shelley. It also houses a full collection of the Keats Shelley Society journals. If you want to further your research into the poets just ask at the desk for access to the locked case where the journals are kept.

As in many museums the curator has been faced with the problem of what to do with a myriad of unrelated items. Here, they are imaginatively displayed in cases called 'A Number of Interesting Things' and 'A Cabinet of Curiosities'. Before you leave this fascinating treasure trove make sure you allow sufficient time to visit the lovely old fashioned walled garden. It's filled with sweet smelling flowers, with its walls displaying old street names from the town.

There's one more place to visit in the town before venturing further away. Continue southwards down The Causeway to St. Mary's Parish Church, completed in 1247. The Shelley family vault is there.

It is now time to journey out of the immediate confines of the town. Two miles southwest, close to the A24, is the small village of Stammerham, home of Christ's Hospital School. It has weathered well and today blends in beautifully with its surroundings but this was not always the case.

In 1902, the year it transferred from London, the critic E V Lucas wrote: "the new Christ's Hospital has been built in the midst of green fields, an arrogant red-brick town which the fastidiously urban ghost of Charles Lamb can never visit".

The Horsham District Heritage Trail Plaque at the visitors entrance to the school, opposite the farm buildings, explains Stammerham means "settlement by the stone lake", in other words, a quarry. The original London building was also used as a quarry, providing some of the stones for the newer Horsham buildings. As in any school, this is private property but guided tours for visitors are sometimes available by arrangement.

Return to the A24 and continue south for 5 miles until you meet a major crossroads. Turn left onto the A272 signposted Haywards Heath. You will see a sign for Pope's Oak Farm. Tradition has it that it was there in 1712, while staying with his friend John Caryll at West Grinstead Park, that **Alexander Pope** wrote 'The Rape of the Lock'. His host could claim some share in the masterpiece, as it was he allegedly who told Pope about a Caryll family feud, the basis for the resulting satire.

There is much to see of literary interest in this small area. West Grinstead Park (bordered by the A24 and A272 - the house has long since disappeared) is now a racehorse breeding centre, part of the National Stud but in the nineteenth century it was the home of **Ernest William Hornung** (always known by his initials E W Hornung). He has two literary claims to fame: one as the begetter of Raffles, the gentleman burglar and two, through his marriage to Connie, as the brother in law of Arthur Conan Doyle, who eventually moved to Crowborough in East Sussex.

One mile from the A24/A272 junction turn into Park Lane. After one more mile it will bring you to the Roman Catholic Church and Shrine of Our Lady of Consolation on the left hand side. One may be surprised to see such an impressive church and the beautiful early 17th century Priest's House in this isolated rural setting.

The Caryll family of West Grinstead, the same landowners who entertained Alexander Pope, were devout Roman Catholics, even in times when this was potentially very dangerous. It was they who endowed the Secret Chapel in what is now the Priest's House. The site became a centre of Catholicism in the area with the present church being built in 1876.

Hilaire Belloc worshipped here frequently when he lived at nearby Shipley. He is buried with his beloved wife Elodie and other members of his family close to the tower door.

The Belloc graves

The tower itself was completed in his memory. Also buried in the churchyard are **Antonia White,** the novelist (best known for 'Frost in May') and James Gunn, the portrait painter.

The church is at a T junction where Park Lane meets the B2135. Turn right onto the B road and the signpost to the Parish Church of St George is immediately visible on the left hand side. Follow the winding lane for about quarter of a mile to the church. Shelley's parents, Timothy and Elizabeth, were married here. Inside the church do make a point of inspecting the names of farms on the backs of pews. They relate to the farms in the parish prior to 1820. It is presumed that the farmers would sit in style here while the rest of their households huddled at the back of the church.

Time now to get back on the road to find where **Hilaire Belloc** lived when in England, although his congenital wanderlust meant he spent much of his life away exploring the byways of Europe. There's scope for more literary tours across the Channel using his book 'A Path to Rome' as a guide. Today, however, is for his beloved Sussex.

Return to the B2135, continuing to skirt West Grinstead Park for another half mile to the junction with the busy A24. Turn right onto it back to the junction with the A272 and this time turn left driving west towards Billingshurst. After about a mile turn left into Pound Lane, signposted three quarters of a mile to Shipley windmill.

Kingsland, the Belloc family home from 1906, is privately owned and not open to the public but the handsome adjacent mill has been restored to working order as a memorial to Belloc by the Shipley Mill Charitable Trust. It is open 2-5 pm on the first and third Sundays in the month from April to October and on Bank Holiday Mondays. Above the door is a tablet which reads: "Let this be a memorial to Hilaire Belloc who garnered a harvest of wisdom and sympathy for young and old". In recent times the windmill has had a new lease of life as the windmill home of the fictional TV hero Jonathon Creek.

After this intensive sightseeing it's time for a late lunch. Return to the A272 and make the short two mile trip westward to Coolham. This tiny village, extending little further than the few buildings round the cross roads, boasts a wonderful pub, The Selsey Arms, a CAMRA pub of the year. You will discover that it is still possible to find a proper old fashioned pub, serving superb simple food at sensible prices. Beside the bar is a framed letter from one customer stating that at his age he expects to be able to complain about services but everything had been so perfect he was left with nothing to grumble about! We agree completely.

When you manage to drag yourself away it's time to return to Horsham. It's only five miles back by the direct route but we're not taking that; there's still another writer to look up today.

Return to the A272 retracing your route easterly. Take the second of the left turnings signposted to Dragons Green and in the village take the right hand fork into Dragons Green Lane, leading to Southwater and nearly back onto the A272.

Wilfrid Blunt's home, Newbuildings Place, where he lived from 1895 until his death in 1922 is on your right hand side. He is buried in the grounds nearby. In 1927 Cunninghame Graham wrote 'Redeemed', an essay about his friend Blunt in which he referred to the bridle path in the woods behind the house where the poet was buried and the great grass mound of the grave between the row of new yew trees, which Blunt had had planted earlier. Today the tomb, with its inscription from Blunt's collected poems of 1914, is overgrown, overshadowed by those very yews, now grown very tall.

Back again to the A24 for the three mile return drive to the centre of Horsham. If you have the appetite for more literary detective work, make a brief diversion onto the A281, which will take you to the home of today's final writer, Georgette Heyer. Blackthorns in Five Oaks Road near Slinfold can be viewed from the drive, although it is obviously private property.

DAY TWO VISIT

If day one's journey was dominated by the A24, today it's the turn of its neighbour, the A29, to take centre stage. But first the A24 has one part to play, Take it to drive northwards out of Horsham town centre. Two miles to the North West, just off the A24, is the small village of Warnham and on its edge is Field Place, **Shelley**'s birthplace.

There are more details about Horsham's brilliant and wayward son in the centre of the village. Opposite the parish church is a village map with a plaque beside it as a further staging post on the Horsham District Heritage Trail.

Today's next port of call is Pulborough ten miles south west of Horsham. Turn south via the A24 to the junction with the A264. Turn right and join the A29. Pulborough played a significant role in **John Wyndham**'s novel 'The Day of the Triffids', the terrifying science fiction account of murderous plants moving across the countryside devouring all in their path.

The novel's hero, Bill Masen, becomes separated from his companions and goes in search of the place of safety, Pulborough, where they had earlier planned to meet. The fictional village is a mile due west of Nutbourne and close to Amberley. With the novel in your hand you can have a fascinating time working out the possible route. You may find yourself glancing over your shoulder from time to time. Don't worry there have been no reports of Triffids in the area for a long time, we think.

The real Amberley is south of Pulborough with a wealth of literary associations in the area. Strangely three significant figures in this area were all born in 1867, although in different months. Continue on the A29 for five miles south through a series of water meadows, turning left at the signpost to Bury. Here is the final home of the first of the 1867 'triplets'. Bury House, **John Galsworthy's** 1910 Tudor style stone house, is immediately visible.

Bury house   *plaque to Galsworthy on the wall*

As the blue plaque states, he lived the last seven years of his life here, writing both 'Swan Song' and 'On Forsyte Change', which completed 'The Forsyte Saga'.

The magnificent house was really too large for Galsworthy and his wife Ada and it was shared with his nephew and his wife. Five gardeners from the village were needed to tend the grounds. Galsworthy had satirised "the man of property" in The Forsyte Saga but ironically that is what he himself had become.

Take the next lane on the left signposted to Houghton and Amberley. This area became a literary centre because of the presence of the Meynells at the beginning of the twentieth century. **Eleanor Farjeon (1881-1965)** first visited the Meynells in 1913 and then bought her own cottage in nearby Houghton. No writer would have dared make up her address of The End Cottage, Mucky Lane!

In time she returned to London but whilst at Houghton she did write 'Martin Pippin in the Apple Orchard', which established her as a children's writer, although some would say she is at least as well known for writing the popular hymn 'Morning Has Broken'.

Continue for half a mile to Amberley. Turn left at the school sign and then into Church Street. Halfway way down on the south side is Boxwood, a double fronted Georgian house with a luxuriant box hedge. The second of the 1867 trio, **Arnold Bennett (1867-1931)** rented Boxwood for a brief two month stay in 1926. Whilst living here he completed his novel 'The Strange Vanguard'. Shortly after his stay he wrote a short story 'The Woman Who Stole Everything' in which Amberley (here renamed Cander) and the surrounding area figure extensively.

Church Street naturally leads to St. Michael's church where an earlier vicar was the father of **Noel Streatfield (1895-1986)**. She was born in Amberley; her father was later appointed to a church in Eastbourne and the Eastbourne chapter contains a much more detailed account of her history.

Amberley Church

The final 1867 triplet, **Arthur Rackham (1867-1939),** with his nightmarish illustrations to Grimms Fairy Stories, lived and worked in Houghton House. He is buried in Amberley churchyard with a memorial plaque on the churchyard wall.

Plaque for Arthur Rackham

From Amberley it is easy to make your way two miles north to Greatham (pronounced Grettam if you want to fit in with the locals). Here on the banks of the river Arun beside the Wild Brooks (a series of water meadows) **Wilfrid** and **Alice Meynell** kept open house for a wide variety of writers, most notably perhaps Francis Thompson. To get there return via Church Street to the High Street then right into East Street, which becomes Rackham Lane. Turn left into Rackham Street and into Greatham Road. Humphrey's Homestead, their eighty acre estate is immediately visible. It is still in the Meynell family.

In 1915 the ever generous Meynells lent one of the estate houses, Shed House, a long low cottage adapted from cowsheds on the Rackham Road to **D.H.Lawrence** when he was completing 'The Rainbow'. While staying there he walked one day with Eleanor Farjeon across the Downs to Chichester, twenty miles away. He felt she was walking much too quickly and told her: "I must teach you to walk like a tramp. You must amble and rest every mile or so". Shed Hall itself was later used by Lawrence as the setting for the title story in his collection 'England, My England'.

Leave Greatham and turn right to join the A 283 going eastwards. The road passes through Storrington where the White Canons Priory is easy to find. Turn south off the High Street and then right into School Lane. The Priory church of Our Lady of England is on your right hand side. The monks here cared for Francis Thompson after Wilfrid Meynell rescued him from vagrancy in London. After a year, Thompson believed himself cured of his opium addiction but it was sadly only a brief respite. Later it was the turn of the Franciscan friars at Crawley Down to attempt what proved, eventually, to be the impossible task of breaking his addiction.

Back to the A283 which passes through Sullington. The popular novelist **A.J.Cronin** (1896-1981) spent some time here when he wrote his best seller 'The Citadel'.

Today was the day for the A29 but not all the time. When you reach the roundabout at Washington take the left hand turn onto the A24, there's no avoiding it, for the direct route back to Horsham.

IF YOU HAVE MORE TIME

This is your opportunity to visit Tennyson's beautiful retreat at Black Down. The poet chose to build his Sussex retreat in a high wind swept setting giving spectacular views over the surrounding area. Like anyone designing a dream home, he agonized long and hard over the possible amenities the house might have.

Surprisingly, for the modern reader, the inclusion of a bathroom was one of the last choices he made. But he didn't regret it. By the end of his life he loved this private sanctum so much he was having three baths a day!

Black Down is five hundred acres of National Trust property but Aldworth House itself is private property and completely hidden from public view by trees planted on the surrounding slopes in Tennyson's time. There is a marked footpath known as 'Tennyson's Walk'.

CAN I DO THESE TOURS WITHOUT A CAR?

Some of the sightseeing outside the town centre could prove a challenge to even the most intrepid visitor without a car but with resourcefulness much can be achieved. The number 23 bus could be your friend. Promisingly, it advertises itself as "A Return to a More Gentle Age" On its way from Horsham to Worthing it passes through Southwater. Details can be found at www.metrobus.co.uk

Slinfold and Southwater are both accessible for cyclists via the Downs Link cycle route. More information about this from: www.nationalcyclenetwork.org.uk

Best of all, the main railway line connects Horsham, Pulborough and Amberley via Christ's Hospital, so consult the National Rail Enquiry Line for further information on 08457 484950.

If you are exploring on foot, bike or even on horseback don't forget to visit www.westsussex.gov.uk/walking for lots of very helpful advice.

BEST TIME TO VISIT

There is so much to see and do here at all times of the year but Horsham, like so many places, probably looks its best in the summer months. Since 1996, it has won many regional, national, and international prizes in bloom competitions and in 2007 was a gold award winner in Britain in Bloom. Floral displays on public spaces and business premises are wonderful and well worth a visit in their own right.

IF YOU HAVE CHILDREN

After visiting Belloc's windmill at Shipley head for Fishers Farm Park off the A272 at Wisborough Green near Billingshurst to solve all your entertainment problems for the under 12s. Details of this superb mixture of farmyard and adventure play can be found at www.fishersfarmpark. co.uk or on 01403700063.

On Day Two you are very close to Amberley Museum and Heritage Centre situated on the B2139. It's a fascinating working museum of industrial history and, as always, don't let that word 'museum' put off the younger members of the party. Take a free nostalgic trip round the site on a vintage bus or a narrow gauge railway and watch rural craftspeople like blacksmiths, wheelwrights and potters demonstrating their age-old skills. More information is at www.amberleymuseum.co.uk or on telephone 01798 831831

Closer to Horsham is Southwater Country Park with its lakeside walks and water sports activities. It's just off the A24: www. horshamdistrictcountryside.org or telephone 01403 731218

LEWES

East Sussex County Town
Rebels and Revolutionaries

LEWES'S WRITERS

Tom Paine (1737-1809)

The father of the American Revolution and author of 'The Rights of Man', which gave rise to the American Declaration of Independence, lived for several years in Lewes. He first arrived in 1768 as the town's new excise officer. He lodged at Bull House in Lewes High Street, a tobacco and grocery shop run by Samuel Ollive.

Paine quickly established himself in the town in spite of his profession - then as now no one wanted to pay taxes. Outside the shop he hung a sign saying: "Every Article of Grocery stocked - Tea excepted" This exception was most significant because even then it reveals Paine's support for the American colonists who were refusing to pay a tax on tea imposed by London. The resulting 'Boston Tea Party' was to demonstrate this most dramatically.

Back in Lewes the family's financial troubles must have seemed to be over when, two years later on the 26th March 1771, Ollive's daughter Elizabeth and Tom were married in St Michael's Church across the High

Street from Bull House. Possibly Tom didn't tell Elizabeth that he had previously been married to a maidservant, Mary Lambert, in Margate in September 1759. She had died less than a year later.

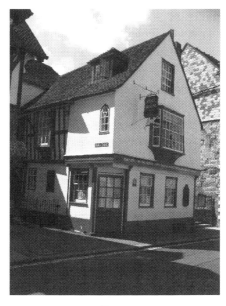

Bull House

This second marriage in Lewes was also short lived and for whatever reason, the couple parted on amicable terms after only three years.

Surely this parting must have been partly occasioned by the stress on Elizabeth living with an idealist who did not seem to recognise that a wife needed the support of a regular income. Paine was dismissed from his job as an excise man as he had made himself highly unpopular with his employers by campaigning to raise the wages of excise men. Rationally he argued that better pay would discourage bribery and so lead to a more efficient public service.

He spent so much time travelling round the country to obtain signatures for a petition to raise wages that his employers were given the perfect excuse to get rid of a difficult employee. He was dismissed in April 1774 for: "having quitted his Business without obtaining the Board's leave".

So once again the spectre of debt hovered over Bull House. Tom and Elizabeth had to sell everything they had to pay off their creditors.

On their legal separation Elizabeth agreed to pay her husband £35 (one imagines this was what was left after all the debts had been settled). Only Bull House itself remained, as this was the property of Samuel Ollive's widow until she died. After her death the property was sold and the proceeds divided between the three children.

Without a wife or a job Tom Paine left Lewes early in 1774, having spent six eventful years there. Later in the same year he left for America where he inspired the 13 Colonies to fight for independence against the British Crown.

THE BLOOMSBURY GROUP – MORE REBELS

At the centre of the group were **Virginia Woolf (1884-1941)** and her sister **Vanessa Bell (1879-1961)**.

The two were brought up in London in the heady intellectual atmosphere that was the home of their widowed father, Leslie Stephens. After his death, writers and artists who had been friends of their brothers at Cambridge would meet at the literary salon the sisters held in their house at 46 Gordon Square, Bloomsbury to talk and develop ideas.

This was to give them the name 'Bloomsbury Group', although this was delightfully but perhaps a little maliciously changed to Bloomsberries by Molly MacCarthy, wife of the literary critic Desmond MacCarthy. Vanessa was to marry one of its members, the literary critic Clive Bell and Virginia another, Leonard Woolf, a writer on politics and economics.

In time, almost the whole Bloomsbury caravan seems to have moved to Sussex, to the area around Lewes, as its members took a series of houses as weekend retreats and boltholes from the pressures of London life. Virginia was the first to arrive. In December 1910 she and her brother Adrian came to Lewes (staying at The Pelham Arms on St Anne's Hill) to do some house hunting.

She had made the decision, supported by her family, that with her delicate mental and physical health she needed to live in the peaceful environment of a country cottage.

Surprisingly, it was not a chocolate-box-roses-round-the-door cottage they chose although, perhaps not surprisingly, as the Bloomsbury Set were never predictable.

Virginia's choice was a newly built villa in the village of Firle, four miles east of Lewes. She named this Little Talland House, after the Stephens' Cornish holiday home. She quickly decided to take a lease on the six year old house, which was to be, for her, the first of four homes in the Lewes area and took up residence in January 1911.

In the following months she entertained many of her fellow 'Bloomsberries', including Leonard Woolf, in what she persisted in calling her "cottage in the South Downs". Virginia had realised early on, what must have been obvious to her family and friends, that however comfortable Little Talland House might be it could never be a suitable expression of her unique personality.

One afternoon in October 1911, as Virginia and Leonard were walking on the Downs near Firle, they found Sussex house number two. It was love at first sight as Virginia glimpsed Asham House, a beautiful Gothic building so unlike the "hideous suburban villa" (at least to Leonard she expressed her true feelings about the house) that was Little Talland.

Shortly afterwards she and Vanessa took it on a shared lease and in February 1912 there was a house warming party. Not warm enough however! It was an unusually cold winter and all the pipes in the house froze.

She and Leonard married in August 1912 at St Pancras Register Office and this was followed by an extensive honeymoon in France, Spain and Italy. While they were away Vanessa Bell moved into Asham House for the winter, arriving at Lewes station with 9 pieces of luggage and a bath! It was Vanessa who made the rather bleak house habitable and when Virginia and Leonard returned to England it became their weekend retreat.

They were frequently to be seen getting off the London train at Lewes station before walking the four miles along the river bank, carrying provisions on their backs in rucksacks. Sadly today Asham House is no more, with the whole area converted into a landfill site. It has, however, been immortalised in Virginia's story "The Haunted House".

Now firmly settled in Sussex it was time for Virginia to go house hunting again, this time for her sister Vanessa, who was living a contentedly Bohemian life in London. She tolerated her husband Clive's mistress, Mary Hutchinson, while she herself was living with the artist Duncan Grant who, in turn, had been the youthful lover of Maynard Keynes.

Virginia and Leonard discovered Charleston Farmhouse, an isolated 17th century building, a few miles from Asham. It was to be the perfect weekend retreat and Vanessa and her family were to spend more and more time there.

The unconventional household took up residence in the autumn of 1916 and immediately set out to transform the old building completely, making it a work of art in itself. Influenced by Post-Impressionists, such as Cezanne and Picasso, they covered the interior with the vivid colours and bright patterns which in time became the hallmark of the Bloomsbury style.

The move to Charleston provided a platform and safe haven while avoiding service in the First World War. In 1916 conscription was introduced for all men between the ages of 18 and 40 years. Clive Bell was exempt on medical grounds. Roger Grant was a Quaker but Duncan Grant and his lover David Garnett became conscientious objectors. Their reasons, rejected at first, were allowed on appeal on the basis that the surrounding land was to be used for food production.

From the moment Vanessa and Duncan moved in, life at Charleston became one long country house party with most of the leading intellectuals of the day signing the visitors' book.

One of the earliest visitors had been the economist **Maynard Keynes (1883-1946)**, who had stayed while writing 'The Economic Consequences of the Peace'. In fact, so regular a visitor had he been that he helped pay the rent.

When he fell in love with the Russian ballerina Lydia Lopokova, he decided he too wanted a country house close to his friends. Tilton seemed to be ideal, just minutes across the fields from Charleston. Sadly the newcomer Lydia was shunned by the clannish Bloomsbury Group: "We prefer reason to any amount of high spirits. Lydia's pranks put us all on edge", wrote Virginia in a letter to one who was still her friend.

Gradually however they all drifted apart and in the late 1930s, while shopping in Lewes, Vanessa did not at first recognise them. Maynard, who suffered from angina, had put on a great deal of weight and Lydia looked "squat and insignificant". Maynard died in 1946 and Lydia stayed at the house until 1977, when she moved to a nursing home in Seaford, dying there in 1981 aged 89. Tilton is now privately owned by Maynard's biographer Robert Skidalsky and is not open to the public.

Virginia and Leonard had their own living problems and in 1919 the lease on Asham House expired. One rumour is that there was an argument between Virginia and Vanessa and that Virginia was under threat of eviction. History repeated itself and, as she had done eight years earlier, she saw and immediately fell in love with what proved to be an unsuitable house.

This one was the Round House in Lewes, only a stone's throw or three from Bull House where, 150 years earlier, Tom Paine had lived.

It became Lewes house number three for her when, on impulse, she paid the estate agent Arthur Wycherley (still a well respected Lewes firm with offices next door to the White Hart Hotel) £300 for the property and went back to London the same day.

White Hart Hotel

Leonard knew nothing of this and some weeks later they both went to visit it and realised it was a dreadful mistake. What they really needed was a much more isolated house. Fate is a strange thing.

On the very day they had returned to inspect the Round House a poster appeared in Lewes announcing the sale by auction of Monks House in Rodmell, a pretty village four miles south of Lewes. This was much more to their taste.

Clearly they were not deterred by its recent history as its previous owner, an old man, had starved himself to death there. Wycherley put the Round House back on the market and instead bid on their behalf for Monks House. The auction took place on the 1st of July 1919 at the White Hart Hotel where Tom Paine and his friends had debated the political issues of the day. Leonard and Virginia paid £700 and became the contented owners of Lewes house number four. This was their last. Monks House became their Sussex retreat for 22 years until Virginia's death in 1941.

Monks House was certainly much smaller and much more primitive than Asham House. At times Virginia's diary reveals that the prospect of another cold weekend at Rodmell would be too depressing and they stayed in London. They were awake at 4am one night chasing mice out of the bed and up again the same night to wedge windows banging in the wind. On another night they caught a bat in the bedroom. But it did become more comfortable.

In 1925 Virginia set herself the target of making £300 in the summer with her writing to build a bath and hot water range there. The masterpiece 'Mrs Dalloway' was the result.

She had a lodge built in the garden where she could write and in 1927 her trips to London were made easier by buying a car. With some of the profits from the Hogarth Press (run from the Woolfs' London home), they were able to buy two cottages in Rodmell for Percy the gardener and Louie the daily help.

After the publication of 'Orlando' they were able to add several rooms to the original farmhouse so that their Bloomsbury friends could visit. There is a fascinating display of photographs today in Virginia's garden study of those house parties. All the great names of 20th century literature are there: T.S.Eliot, E.M.Forster, Aldous Huxley, Lytton Strachey and Vita Sackville-West and there was constant coming and going between Charleston and Monks House.

In the 20 years she and Leonard spent at Monks House together Virginia was constantly writing novels, diaries and essays. Across the river there was similar great professional success for the artistic community at Charleston. Their artistry found one unexpected outlet in a bold move by George Bell, the Bishop of Chichester, a great patron of the arts, who commissioned Duncan Grant and Vanessa Bell to cover the interior of nearby Berwick church with murals.

Berwick Church

They were first commissioned shortly after the Bishop took office in 1929 but such a controversial plan took a long time to implement. The work was finally begun in 1941, when Vanessa's children Quentin and Angelica also helped with the task. The artists combined familiar Bible stories with portraits of local people in the foreground and Sussex views in the background.

In 1941, while plans were afoot to decorate Berwick church, a few miles away Virginia fell into a deep depression unlike anything Leonard had seen before. She had just finished 'Between the Acts', where two of her Sussex homes in Rodmell and Firle form the backdrop for the action. Finishing a novel was always a dangerous time for her mental health. On the 28th of March Leonard had been working in the garden. He went into lunch and found a letter waiting for him:

"Dearest

I feel certain that I am going mad again. I feel we can't go through another of those terrible times and I shan't recover this time. I begin to hear voices and I can't concentrate. So I am doing what seems the best thing to do".

He found her walking stick on the banks of the River Ouse a few minutes walk from the house. Three weeks later a group of boys playing by the river further downstream discovered her body. She had put heavy stones into her pocket before wading into the river.

Strangely the spot where she entered the water was almost opposite Asham House, the earlier and final Sussex homes forming a sad symmetry. Her body was cremated in Brighton and Leonard buried her ashes in the garden of Monks House.

His own ashes were buried beside Virginia after his death in 1969 and the house was then owned for ten years by Sussex University, at one time being let to Saul Bellow when he was Visiting Professor. Today the property is owned by The National Trust.

Siegfried Sassoon (1886-1967)

Sassoon grew up in Kent but through his friendship with Norman Loder of the Southdown Hunt - based just outside Ringmer - he became a regular visitor to this part of the world. He stayed in the rectory at East Hoathley (again very close to Ringmer, just off the A22) where the rector, the Rev'd Harry Harboard, was a keen huntsman.

When war was declared in 1914 Sassoon, like most young men of his generation and class, saw a chance to extend the thrills and dangers of the hunting field to a nobler cause. It was only when he reached the trenches that dreadful reality dawned. He must have set some kind of record as one of the first in the country to enlist. On the 4th of August, the very day that war was declared, he signed on in Lewes Drill Hall with C Company of the Sussex Yeomanry. At 28 years old he was getting very close to the upper age limit of 30 for volunteers.

He spent the next two nights sleeping on the floor of Lewes Corn Exchange before moving with the rest of the Yeomanry to their tented camp on the Downs outside Lewes. He quickly realised, however, that the cavalry had had their day and changed his allegiance to the infantry, gaining a commission with the Royal Welch Fusiliers thus marking the end of his close connection with the Lewes area.

ONE DAY VISIT

The railway station, with its convenient car park, makes a good starting point. Just a five minute walk from it up Station Street (be warned, it's quite steep like most roads in Lewes) brings you to the High Street, where all the major buildings associated with Tom Paine are situated very close together. A leisurely morning's stroll will take in all these sites.

Immediately on your left is The White Hart Hotel. Paine was a founder member of the aptly named Headstrong Club, where educated Lewesians met to debate the issues of the day. He quickly established himself as one of the liveliest of the Club's debaters putting forward very advanced views, for the 1790s, on the abolition of slavery and the need for international arbitration instead of war.

It was here too in 1919 that **Virginia** and **Leonard Woolf** bought Monks House by auction. Wycherleys Estate Agents, who acted for them, is still next door.

Three hundred metres further down on the left is Bull House. You can't miss the fact that Paine lived here. Its written right across the whole of its façade. No genteel plaque for this revolutionary! The house is now owned by the Sussex Archaeological Society, with offices on the ground floor and part of the first floor. The rest is private property.

Continue for thirty metres and Keere Street is on your left hand side.

Be prepared for the cobbles. This is probably where **Eve Garnett (1900–1991)** set her 'Family from One End Street'. She lived in Lewes for over fifty years, first at 116 High Street, which you have passed on this morning's tour and later in Keere Street at number 12. Going down this very steep hill is easy but the return trip is hard work. One pities the horses of the Prince Regent (the son of George III) which, tradition has it, were raced here for a wager. The bottom of the street will bring you to Southover Grange, a beautiful Elizabethan house built in 1572.

Keere Street

The diarist **John Evelyn (1620-1706)** spent much of his childhood here in what was then his grandmother's house. You may even have come across a description of it already since it appeared as 'Mock Beggar Hall' in **William Harrison Ainsworth's (1805-1882)** popular historical novel 'Ovingdean Grange - A Tale of the South Downs', written during his fifteen year stay in Brighton.

Refresh yourself with a gentle walk through its walled garden, a peaceful oasis right in the middle of town before you return to the High Street. Rather than making the slow and steep ascent up Keere Street, continue left beside Southover Grange until you come to the appropriately named Paine's Passage. Eventually this will bring you back to Bull House.

If you feel energised by this walk, make a half mile detour. Turn left along what is now St Anne's Hill (yes, the clue is in the name; Lewes is a town of hills but at least what goes up must come down). This in its turn becomes Western Road. Pass St Anne's church on your left and turn left at the traffic lights into St. Anne's Crescent. Here at number 44 (Southdown House) lived **Daisy Ashford (1881-1972)** who at an amazing 9 years old wrote 'The Young Visitors'.

This amusing, albeit unpunctuated, insight into upper class life in the town remained in a drawer for almost 30 years and some then doubted whether such a confident satire could be such a young child's work. An early doubter was J.M.Barrie, but once convinced of the writer's authenticity he wrote an introduction to the first edition.

Return the way you came to Bull House. Immediately across the road is St Michael's Church, where Tom Paine and Elizabeth Ollive were married in March 1771. It has an unusual round tower, one of only three such towers in Sussex, the other two being at nearby Southease and Piddinghoe. Next to the church is Pipe Passage and a one minute walk down it will bring you to the Round House, briefly owned by Virginia Woolf. Today it is a private residence.

Turn back to the High Street and continue towards the White Hart Hotel. Before you reach it, turn left into Castle Precinct at the Norman Castle, built immediately after the Norman Conquest. Within its precincts lies the original tilting green, used by Lewes Bowling Green Society since 1753.

Here, 15 years later, Thomas Paine became a very accomplished player who "observed much more exactness with the measuring stick than he was accustomed to do at the beer-barrel with his dipping–rule". Continue along Castle Precinct and cross over Fisher Street into Market Lane. You will see a car park and the Needlemakers Centre on your left. The many craft shops that fill this centre are always worth a visit.

Veer right at the Crown Hotel and into the Market Tower, built in 1792 as a provision market but now merely a short cut into the High Street.

Today its main feature is a dramatic portrait of Tom Paine painted by Julian Bell, grandson of Vanessa, in 1994. It shows Paine with an upraised arm pointing west to America whilst below him is Lewes including the river Ouse where the painter's great aunt, Virginia Woolf, drowned. Over Paine's right shoulder can be seen the Bastille burning, marking the start of the French Revolution. There is an inspiring quotation from Paine's own writing beneath: "We have it in our power to build the world anew".

Finally, turn right into the High Street where you will find Lewes Tourist Office on your right. The friendly and knowledgeable staff are waiting to answer all your questions. By now you'll be ready for a break. It's time for lunch.

Market Tower

If you feel a liquid lunch is called for, order a pint of the rightly celebrated local Harveys beer. John Harvey, founder of the Bridge Wharf Brewery was born just 10 years after Tom Paine left the town. The two never met but the brewery does much to keep Paine's memory alive. Since 1993 (appropriately on the 4th of July) Harveys has brewed Tom Paine Ale in the great man's honour. The Strong Pale Ale is available in several pubs in Lewes.

The afternoon is time for some more literary history. You may want to trace other fathers of American independence. Two miles NE from Lewes (on B2192) is the village of Ringmer, now growing with new estates to accommodate Lewes workers and London commuters looking for some rural peace. Head first to the pretty medieval church, dedicated to St Mary.

Inside the church are the Springett memorials to the original Lords of the Manor. In 1643 it was to St. Mary's that his brother officers brought the body of Sir William Springett, a Roundhead, after he died in the Siege of Arundel during the English Civil War. He was only 23. His posthumous daughter Giuliema became the wife of the Quaker, William Penn, the founder of Pennsylvania.

Another Ringmer connection with America is Ann, the daughter of the Rev'd John Sadler, vicar here between 1620 and 1640. She married John Harvard who went on to found the great university. Strangely, her marriage was not in her home church of Ringmer but two miles away, in Malling Church in Lewes.

Close to the village green is Delves House, now divided into flats. It was here that a third famous Ringmer resident lived - not another early GI Bride but a tortoise! **Gilbert White**, the 18th century Hampshire parson-naturalist, paid an annual visit to his aunt, Mrs Rebecca Snooke, who lived there. Timothy, a venerable tortoise, lived among the yew hedges and mulberry trees (some are still there today) and came like a dog to be fed when Mrs. Snooke called him. Her nephew was clearly very fond of the animal and documented its habits in great detail in letters and diaries.

In April 1772 he described a recent visit in a letter to a friend: "I was much taken with its sagacity in discerning those who do it kind offices; for, as soon as the good old lady comes in sight who has waited on it for more than thirty years, it hobbles towards its benefactress with awkward alacrity, but remains inattentive to strangers".

Sign with Timothy and others

When Mrs Snooke died Gilbert White took the tortoise back to Selbourne where its life was fully documented in 'The Natural History of Selbourne'. Timothy's carapace can now be seen in the Natural History collection at the British Museum in London. As you return to Lewes, look back at the village sign at the entrance to Ringmer where Vicarage

Way joins the main Lewes Road. There, in the middle, is Timothy, immortalised together with the other village worthies: William Penn, Guiliema Springett, John Harvard and Ann Sadler.

TWO DAY VISIT

You are now ready to tackle The Bloomsbury Trail. Be warned, there's a lot to see and an early start is advised. You also need to check opening times at individual properties, as they do not necessarily coincide. We suggest Wednesdays and Saturdays in the summer months will ensure all properties are open to visitors. Since Monks House does not open until the afternoon this trail goes to other houses first.

The easiest, though not the only, way to follow the trail is by car so you may need some food to sustain you. Both Bill's Produce Store in Cliffe High Street and Crumbs on School Hill are local institutions easily accessible from the railway station or the White Hart hotel. Any local will point you in the right direction to them.

Once you have stocked up on provisions leave Lewes via the Cuilfail Tunnel and drive east on the A27. Your first stop will be a huge disappointment. At Beddingham roundabout turn right on to the A26 (signs to Newhaven). One mile along on the left hand side is the entrance to Beddingham Landfill Site. It is all that remains of Asham House. It was near here in the River Ouse that Virginia's body was discovered.

Ironically, her final home at Rodmell is directly opposite Asham on the other side of the Ouse. Return to the A27 via the Beddingham roundabout and continue east (turning right) for about a mile or so. The turn off for Firle village is on the right hand side. Firle is as cut off today from the rush of modern life as it was in Virginia Woolf's time. It is dominated by Firle Place, the beautiful Elizabethan home of Viscount Gage.

The first Viscount's second son commanded the British forces at the outbreak of the American War of Independence. One could hazard a guess as to what Tom Paine thought of his aristocratic Lewes neighbour! A later Viscount Gage introduced the green plum, the greengage, to England.

Drive down the winding main street of the village and find Talland

House on the left hand side opposite the village hall. It is one of a pair of brick houses with the date 1904 above the door. It is a private residence and closed to the public. In the north east corner of the village churchyard, beside the church, will be found the simple headstones marking the graves (see below) of Vanessa Bell and Duncan Grant.

Graves of Vanessa Bell and Duncan Grant

Return to the A27 and continue east. You are actually making for Charleston Farmhouse but may be interested in a brief diversion to see where the tormented novelist **Malcolm Lowry (1909-1957)** lived and died.

Turn left after two miles, just before Middle Farm, down the lane signposted to Ripe and Laughton. The winding lane turns into The Street and the centre of Ripe village. Veer right at the village centre past the Lamb Inn. Lowry was banned from here after a violent incident.

The village church is straight ahead and the novelist's grave is opposite the west door of the tower, behind the low flint wall. Margerie Lowry is not buried with her husband but on the left side of the church door, as far away from him as she could be! To the left of the church, the lane leads to The White Cottage where Lowry lived for the final year of his life. This is where he died in somewhat mysterious circumstances.

Return the way you came to the A27 (turning left) and drive past Middle Farm on your left. Charleston Farmhouse is signposted on the right hand side. You will find a winding single track lane, fortunately with passing places, leading to the house and beautiful walled garden. Charleston is open from mid March to the end of October on Wednesdays to Sundays between 11.30am to 6.00pm and Thursdays and Fridays from 2.00pm to 6.00pm. Entry is by guided tour lasting approximately one hour but we do strongly recommend the more detailed Sisters Tour lasting 90 minutes, available on some Fridays.

Only a few hundred metres away and very near to the footpath leading east then south from Charleston is Maynard Keynes's home at Tilton. Both the track and the farmhouse itself are private property.

Go back again to the A27. By now you will be getting to know this road rather well. This particular stretch has seen far too many accidents and the right turn onto it from Charleston requires vigilance. Drive another two miles east when you will see a signpost to the village of Berwick on your right. The church is at the end of the village. You may notice an old pub on this road, The Cricketers Arms, where the seeds for this book were sown in the cosy dining room by the open fire.

Cricketers Arms

Berwick Church is at the end of the road. By now you should be able to recognise some of the local views depicted in its murals.

Notice especially the Nativity painting by Vanessa Bell on the north wall. The barn is modelled on the one at Tilton and in the background is Mount Caburn, near Lewes, clearly visible from the A27. A good deal of financial backing for the work came from Peter Jones, the department store owner, whilst John Christie of Glyndebourne provided the enormous easels for the plasterboard panels. Thus the artists were able to paint in comfort in their own studio at Charleston. The finished murals were fixed to the walls of the church in January 1943 and were dedicated by Bishop Bell in October 1943.

There is one remaining Bloomsbury property to see and many would say it is the most evocative of them all. Go back to the A27 turning left and retrace your route. Bypass Lewes and continue to the next roundabout. Turn left through the village of Kingston and join the C7 at Wyevale Garden Centre. Turn right and continue south for 4 miles to Rodmell and then turn left into the main street at the Abergavenny Arms.

Monks House is half a mile along and the last building on the right hand side of the High Street but it is best to drive past to park in the National Trust car park at the very end of the street. The property is owned by the National Trust with a custodian in residence. It opens at 2.00pm on Wednesday and Saturday afternoons from the 1st of April until the end of October. As befits its religious name (although historians now doubt whether monks ever did inhabit the house) the house is next door to the church. Once again Virginia may have chosen a less than perfect location since she actually loathed the sound of church bells, dismissing them as "intermittent, sullen and didactic".

Much of the house is as it was when the Woolfs lived there. It is long and narrow with the main entrance through the full length greenhouse built on the south side. After the exuberant colour of Charleston the rooms appear rather dark. They are quite small with the downstairs sitting room decorated in Virginia's favourite sea green. It is a joy to come out into the lush gardens designed by Leonard Woolf and frequently altered by him, to the despair of Percy Bartholomew, the gardener.

Now only one part of this literary pilgrimage remains. The exact spot where Virginia ended her life is not marked but from available evidence a lot can be deduced. Leave Monks House and turn right passing on your right two garages built by Leonard Woolf for his employees and then into the National Trust car park. A bridleway leads down through a copse of sycamores and willows to water meadows beside the River Ouse.

A wartime pillbox can still be seen, a reminder of Virginia's darkest fear of a German invasion starting with a spearhead contingent advancing from the south coast. She probably had good cause for this fear in the dark days of 1940/41. Rodmell is certainly very close to the port of Newhaven. Virginia must have picked up stones on her last sad walk and entered the water at this spot.

As Leonard and fellow villagers spent the afternoon in a desperate search of the village and the area around the streams, they found Virginia's walking stick in the mud and her footprints leading into the water. It was to be three weeks before her body was found by children playing by the river about two miles from the cement wharf at Beddingham, where Asham House had stood. After this it will be a sombre drive back to the welcoming lights of Lewes.

CAN I DO THESE TOURS WITHOUT A CAR?

Day One tour of Lewes is certainly best completed on foot. Ringmer is a 10 minute taxi ride away. Day Two Bloomsbury Trail is more challenging but remember the Bloomsberries used to tramp and cycle all over the Sussex countryside visiting each other. If they could do it so can you!

On a seven mile walk you can see most of the major sites. If you begin at Lewes Railway Station a 10 minute taxi ride will easily take you to Rodmell and Monks House. Walk through the school playground past the church to the River Ouse. Follow the raised bank to the swing bridge at Southease then cross this, the railway line and the main Newhaven road. Soon you will be opposite the site of Asham House.

Head over the escarpment on the South Downs Way and drop down to West Firle village to see Vanessa Bell's and Duncan Grant's graves and Little Talland House. Return to the footpath that twists around Firle Beacon for a glimpse of Tilton Farmhouse. A left turn will bring you to a farm track leading west, then north to Charleston itself.

An even nicer way to see some of the properties is by courtesy of the Cuckmere Community Bus. The first bus on Saturdays on Route 25 leaves Lewes Railway Station at 9.43am before going to Firle village, Charleston Farmhouse and Berwick. With careful planning it should be possible to do the round trip before returning to Lewes Station at approximately 5.33pm.

BEST TIME TO VISIT

It really depends on whether or not you like fireworks. This quiet town explodes every 5th of November (always referred to in Lewes as 'Bonfire'), when no fewer than five separate firework celebrations take place in the town. Everything stops by 4.00pm. Shops close and board up their windows if they are on one of the processional routes. Those who work outside the town hurry back to beat the road blocks as the town becomes sealed off from the outside world from 5.00 pm until midnight.

Much is being commemorated and the reason for most of it is lost in the mists of time. Some historians suggest we are witnessing a folk memory of the prehistoric fires which marked the beginning of the Celtic New Year. Certainly events half a century before the Guy Fawkes' Gunpowder Plot are also being remembered.

Seventeen Lewes Protestants were executed for their faith during the reign of Queen Mary Tudor, Henry VIII's elder daughter. If you do decide to go to Lewes on the 5th get there early to get a good vantage point on the High Street to see the processions and make sure you book your hotel room beforehand. There's no room at the inns on the night itself.

Every May under the umbrella of the nearby Brighton Festival (more detail on this in the Brighton chapter), Charleston has its own literary festival where authors show case their work. Tickets for both festivals are available online at:

www.charleston.org.uk and www.brightonfestival.org.

Lewes is an excellent centre to stay for visiting Glyndebourne opera.

IF YOU HAVE CHILDREN

Five miles from Lewes on the left hand side of the A27, just past the road to Firle, is Middle Farm, a working farm where the whole family can wander round happily before the youngsters are let loose in the imaginatively designed Adventure Playground. At 3.00pm visitors are encouraged to go into the Milking Parlour to see the herd of Jersey cows being milked. The award-winning Farm Shop sells local farm produce and baked goods from its own kitchen. It would make another good place to stock up on picnic food.

After visiting Charleston and Berwick Church, a very short diversion further east along the A27 will bring you to Drusillas (turn right off the roundabout – 3rd exit), which is widely regarded as the best small zoo in the country. Go to www.drusillas.co.uk (01323 874100) for more details.

RYE and HASTINGS

The Far East of East Sussex

⟹◆⟸

RYE AND HASTING'S WRITERS

John Fletcher (1579-1625)

Rye proudly claims John Fletcher as its own, although he actually left the town when he was only 2 years old. He is best known as half of the 16th century script writing team of Beaumont and Fletcher producing, among other works, 'The Maid's Tragedy'. The pair became the most successful partnership in Elizabethan playwriting and they were certainly more popular in their day than a certain Stratford-upon-Avon dramatist. His father, Rye vicar Richard Fletcher, was a prominent churchman who eventually became Bishop of London and attended the execution of Mary Queen of Scots.

LAMB HOUSE AND ITS THREE WRITERS

Lamb House

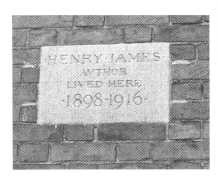

Plaques recording Henry James

Lovely Lamb House, named after wine merchant James Lamb, who built it in 1723, has been home successively to several writers, including Henry James, E.F. Benson and Rumer Godden. It had its own narrative even before their arrival. In the winter of 1726, King George I, returning to England from Hanover, was forced to stay for four nights there after his ship was driven onto nearby Camber Sands during a storm. The bad weather continued and he was then snowed in. He wasn't the only arrival

- during his stay Lamb's wife gave birth to a son and the king agreed to be his godfather. The child was, of course, christened George.

Henry James (1843-1916)

American born Europhile Henry James had already spent twenty two years in London before he made the move to Sussex. His literary reputation had been made by such novels as 'The Portrait of a Lady', and 'Washington Square' but his novel 'The Bostonians' had a much cooler review from the critics, as did his play 'Guy Domville'.

Always one to be stung by criticism, James left London for Rye hoping for a more sympathetic and calmer environment. He was to remain in the town for the next eighteen years until his death in 1916, although towards the end of his life he stayed in London to escape the cold winters in Rye. He first lived at The Old Vicarage, where he wrote 'The Spoils of Poynton' and moved to Lamb House in 1898. Here in the Green Room, or in warmer weather in the Garden Room, looking out on to Rye's cobbled streets, he dictated his last three important novels: 'The Wings of the Dove', 'The Ambassadors' and 'The Golden Bowl'.

E.F.Benson (1867-1940)
(And his brother A C Benson 1862-1925)

Plaque on the wall of Lamb House
garden for the Benson brothers.

These two literary brothers were the sons of Edward White Benson, Archbishop of Canterbury from 1882 but perhaps more significantly for young boys, Headmaster of Wellington College where they were brought up and then educated.

Although Fred Benson is the better known and is, in fact, the raison d'être for a visit to Rye for many people, his younger brother, Arthur Christopher, was also a prolific writer. His novels never achieved the success that his brother's did but he has his own claim to fame. He wrote the words of 'Land of Hope and Glory' to the music of Elgar's 'Pomp and Circumstance March No.1'.

Edward Frederic Benson's first visit to Rye was to stay with the family friend Henry James at Lamb House. The house must have made a great impression as shortly after James' death in 1916 he moved into part of the building. He took over the full lease in 1920 with his brother Arthur, who spent time there on vacation from his university work as Vice-Master of Magdalene College, Cambridge.

Although he was a prolific writer, producing more than 100 novels, memoirs and biographies, it is the six Mapp and Lucia books which formed Fred Benson's reputation. Four of these witty, sharp eyed observations of English country town life in the 1920s ('Miss Mapp', 'Mapp and Lucia', 'Lucia's Progress' and 'Trouble for Lucia') are set in Rye.

He renamed Rye and called it Tilling after the nearby river Tillingham. Miss Elizabeth Mapp and Mrs Emmeline 'Lucia' Lucas jointly own Mallards (based closely on Lamb House) and use the Garden Room to spy on Tilling/Rye society – just as their creator was doing!

Fred Benson loved Rye and the people of Rye loved him. After Arthur's death he spent most of his time here, becoming a local magistrate and then mayor for three years between 1934 and 1937. After his death from throat cancer in February 1940 in University College Hospital, London, his body was brought back to his beloved Rye where he was buried in the town cemetery.

Rumer Godden (1907-1998)

This part of Sussex had special significance for Rumer Godden. She had been educated at Moira House, the prestigious girls' school along the coast in Eastbourne. In the early sixties she spent time at Little Doucegrove, Northiam, the former home of Sheila Kaye-Smith. She lived at Lamb House between 1967 and 1974 documenting her stay in the second volume of her autobiography 'The House with Four Rooms'.

An even more charming record of her stay is the children's picture book: 'A Kindle of Kittens', with its evocative illustrations by Lynne Byrnes. The book delightfully describes a stray tabby cat's determination to find good homes for her three kittens in a nameless old town, which is clearly Rye.

All three are given good homes by the townspeople with one being taken in at Lamb House, here renamed the Mansion House. Although Rumer Godden died in Scotland, her ashes were buried with her husband's in Rye.

OTHER RYE WRITERS

Stephen Crane (1871-1900)

Stephen Crane's brief stay in Sussex began in 1899, though he and his partner, Cora, had first arrived in England two years earlier. Crane was employed as a war correspondent but it was his fictional account of the American Civil War in 'The Red Badge of Courage' which brought him immense fame on both sides of the Atlantic. In spite of large royalties from the book, the Cranes were always short of money, partly because they entertained so lavishly.

They were given Brede Place, in Brede near Rye, by wealthy friends, living there rent free.

Entrance to Brede Place

It was certainly a generous offer and one should not look a gift horse in the mouth but the draughty, medieval manor house was the worst place to live for someone in Crane's precarious state of health. He was riddled with tuberculosis and added to this he smoked too much and ate too little. One of the Cranes many concerned friends, fellow American Henry James, cycled over from his home in nearby Rye two or three times a week to check on the pair's well being.

At the Cranes' Christmas party at Brede Place in 1899, Stephen collapsed with a haemorrhage. H.G.Wells, one of the guests, immediately cycled off to summon medical aid. This was the last Crane was to see of Brede Place. Cora took her beloved Stephen to Europe in search of a better climate, hoping that there his health would improve. First stop was the Black Forest. It was too late, however, and on the fifth of June, 1900 he died. His body was taken back home to New Jersey for burial in the family grave.

Sheila Kaye-Smith (1887-1956)

Sheila Kaye-Smith is probably the most successful Sussex novelist in conveying that elusive sense of place about the county. Almost all her life was spent in Sussex and her intense love for its people and places pervades all her writing.

Born in Hastings in Battle Lodge, Dane Road in 1887, the daughter of a local doctor, she had her first literary success with her novel 'The Tramping Methodist' in 1908 when she was only 21. This led to a spate of novels with Sheila Kaye Smith being able to produce one every six to nine months.

In 1921 came the one that gave her lasting fame. 'Joanna Godden', (later made into a film), is a story of the Romney Marshes with much of the action taking place in Rye.

Allied with her love of Sussex was her deep religious faith. It was Anglo-Catholicism which first attracted her and she found a natural home in Christ Church, St. Leonard's where, in 1928, she married the curate, Penrose Fry.

The previous year had seen the publication of 'The House of Alard' which became an overnight success on both sides of the Atlantic. The Alards were an actual Sussex family whose history went back many centuries. There are ancestral tombs in Winchelsea Church and the family home of Conster Manor was close to her own later home at Doucegrove.

The years immediately following her marriage saw her brief exile from her beloved county. Her husband became a curate in a large London church in Kensington but both she and Penrose had long felt a call to leave the Catholic wing of the Church of England and convert to Roman Catholicism. Penrose resigned his curacy in 1929 so they were then free to return to her favourite part of her favourite county.

They bought an isolated oast house, Little Doucegrove, situated between Northiam and Brede and shortly afterwards both were received into the Roman Catholic Church. The nearest Catholic Church was 9 miles away in Rye so the Frys converted a stable loft into an oratory called The Upper Room, with a priest coming in from Rye to celebrate a weekly Mass for Catholics in the surrounding area. As the congregation steadily increased The Upper Room became too small and Sheila and her husband paid for a small church dedicated to St. Therese of Lisieux to be built in the grounds of Little Doucegrove.They are both buried in its churchyard.

John Ryan (1921-2009)

On a lighter note, one must not forget John Ryan's creation, Captain Pugwash. His swashbuckling adventures have brought pleasure to countless children. The Cinque Port of Rye, his creator's hometown, becomes Sinkport in many of the stories.

WRITERS IN HASTINGS

John Keats (1795-1821)

As Hastings has spread westwards it has swallowed up Bo-Peep, the delightfully named hamlet where young and restless John Keats (he was only 22) stayed for little more than a week in 1817.

It was a highly significant time for him as he met there another summer visitor, Isabella Jones. He fell deeply in love and immortalised her as a nymph in Book 2 of 'Endymion' where she rises naked from The Fishponds, a local beauty spot. Eighteen months later they met by chance in London and renewed their acquaintance. It seems likely that this time, after staying with her before his journey to Chichester, she provided the model for Madeline in 'The Eve of St Agnes' (see the chapter about Chichester for more details about the writing of this poem).

Rider Haggard (1856-1925)

Sir Henry Rider Haggard had already become a best selling writer of adventure stories such as 'King Solomon's Mines' and 'Allan Quartermain' when he came to Sussex. His main homes were in Norfolk and London, but the cold winters of the former and the fogs of the latter made life difficult for someone who had spent his formative years in South Africa as a colonial administrator. Towards the end of his life he increasingly spent the winter in the comfort of his brother's house in St. Leonards. This town, close to more ancient Hastings, was founded in the 1820s as a fashionable seaside resort.

In all, Rider Haggard wrote 34 adventure stories set in a variety of exotic landscapes including Ancient Egypt, Mexico and Constantinople but it is his African stories which have enduring appeal. They are so clearly written by one who had a very close knowledge of African wildlife, its landscape and tribal society.

Robert Tressell (1868-1911)

He should more accurately be called Robert Noonan, the pen name 'Tressell' was chosen as a tribute to his fellow workers - professional decorators use a trestle table.

His early life was spent in South Africa, where he learnt to be a house painter and sign writer. After an acrimonious divorce and the horrors of the Boer War, South Africa had lost its appeal and he and his young daughter joined his sister's family in Hastings.

Here he earned his living as a decorator at the same time writing his masterpiece novel, 'The Ragged Trousered Philanthropists', which highlights the dreadful working conditions of labourers in Hastings (which he renamed Mugsborough) at the beginning of the twentieth century.

It took him five years to complete and at the end of that time his health was broken, having suffered from tuberculosis for many years. He left for Liverpool hoping to emigrate from there to Canada with his eighteen year old daughter as soon as he was well enough to make the journey. But this was not to be. He died in Liverpool and was buried in an unmarked pauper's grave. Kathleen, his daughter, sold the manuscript to a publisher and it was first published posthumously in 1914 in a shortened form.

ONE DAY VISIT

We suggest today is given over to exploring Rye. Obviously a visit to Lamb House is crucial so your visit needs to be planned around its opening times. As it is a National Trust property it follows the normal seasonal opening times of mid-March to October. It is well worth noting, however, that it is open for just two days a week, on Thursday and Saturday afternoons between 2.00pm and 6.00pm. There is so much of literary interest to see in Rye and district that your morning will be well filled before Lamb House opens for business.

If you are making Rye your base, it would be a good idea to leave it to visit sites connected with **Sheila Kaye-Smith** in the morning.

Take the B2089 out of Rye in the direction of Broad Oak, passing through Udimore. After seven miles you will reach Broad Oak and there turn left (south) on the A28. Drive via Cackle Street the one mile or so to Brede.

The church is well worth a visit. Don't miss the lovely Virgin and Child carved in oak by author and sculptor, **Clare Sheridan**, a cousin of Winston Churchill. She, like Stephen Crane, was a later occupant of Brede Place.

Brede Place itself is in Stubb Lane, opposite the church. Drive along for exactly one mile. Don't give up! The lane is very pretty but gives the impression it leads nowhere. The Gate House to Brede Place is on the right hand side of the lane. Both it and Brede Place itself are private property.

The next stop is Doucegrove Farm, with its associations with Sheila Kay-Smith. Return to the A28 at Brede and turn right (north). Follow the road through Cackle Street and Broad Oak. After about two and a half miles you will pass on your right Conster Manor, the family home of the Alards in 'The End of the House of Alards'. A further mile on you will see a sign pointing to 'Catholic Church'. Turn right into Rocks Hill and you are at Doucegrove Farm.

In front of you lies the small group of buildings that make up the Doucegrove estate. Sheila Kaye-Smith's house is at the end of the lane with a row of cottages and a stable, now a garage, at the entrance. Above this was the Upper Room. All is private property. The Catholic Church, dedicated to her favourite saint, St. Therese of Lisieux, is on the left of the lane. She and her husband lie side by side beneath an impressive graveyard crucifix.

Their graves are identically simple, with an apt quotation from The Book of Proverbs describing a good wife, marking where the writer was laid to rest. "She hath considered a field and bought it; with the fruit of her hand she hath planted a vineyard".

To return to Rye, rejoin the A28 turning right (north). After about half a mile, turn right on to the B2165 for Beckley, where you meet the A268. Turn right here and continue into Rye (6 miles) passing through Peasmarsh where Beatle Paul McCartney has his farm.

Time now to explore Rye. It is a Cinque Port. In spite of the Norman French for five, there were actually seven ancient towns which traditionally provided ships to guard the king and his armies before the formation of a national maritime force (which eventually became the Royal Navy). Nearby Hastings was another member of this confederation and has an equally blood stained past defending the coastline. There is less for Rye to defend today as the sea retreated from the town centuries ago and now is almost two miles away.

You certainly don't need a car in Rye. It is a small town with a population of only 5000 and is easily explored on foot. Do be warned, however. The historical centre is set on a hill and its cobbled streets can present a challenge to high heels. The town is well provided with car parks and the one on the Hastings side of the town towards the West is the most convenient (pay and display but free on Sundays).

Try to visit the Tourist Information Centre on Strand Quay at the beginning of your visit. This has a very good selection of maps and guides but also houses the Rye Town Model Sound and Light Show, which brings to life 700 years of Rye history.

You are now ready to tackle those cobbles by walking up Wish Ward to Mermaid Street. In Benson's Tilling this kept its nautical flavour but was renamed Porpoise Street. On the corner stands The Mermaid Inn which was rebuilt in 1420 following the French raid on the town in 1377.

Mermaid Inn

Much of Rye was burnt to the ground in the attack and even today there are areas of stone in the church which are reddened from the fires. In the 18th century The Mermaid Inn became the headquarters of the Hawkhurst Gang, one of the most feared bands of smugglers on the south coast. It has appeared in many smuggling stories. **Richard Aldington (1892-1962)**, the poet and novelist, lived here for a time and it appears in his 1929 novel 'Death of a Hero'.

Mermaid Street is full of beautiful old buildings, many with very unusual names such as 'The House Opposite' and 'The House with the Seat' and 'The House With Two Front Doors'. Jeake's House is here, a very popular Bed and Breakfast establishment.

Jeake's House

Plaque for Conrad Aiken

This former Quaker Meeting House was bought by the American poet and novelist **Conrad Aiken** in 1924, the year he wrote an introduction to a collection of Emily Dickinson's poetry. Jeake's House is equally as old as Lamb House but somewhat smaller. It too became a centre for literary visitors. **Malcolm Lowry** spent his vacations from Cambridge here with Aiken and his family. His novel 'Ultramarine', published in 1929, owes much to Aiken's 'Blue Voyage' of 1927.

Lamb House (rechristened Mallards by Benson in his Mapp and Lucia novels) is at the corner of Mermaid Street and West Street.

In his autobiography **H.G.Wells**, a frequent visitor, wrote that it was "one of the most perfect pieces of suitably furnished Georgian architecture imaginable" and it is very easy to concur with this view. Passing through the dignified front door one finds four downstairs rooms which hold a wealth of literary mementos, principally reflecting Henry James' stay. Sadly the Garden Room is no more.

Almost a small house in itself, it was destroyed by German bombs in 1940. One can still have a good idea of the view it enjoyed (and chances to spy on townspeople that both James and Benson appreciated) by looking through the window of the Oak Parlour, which was placed next to the Garden Room at the front of the house.

The beautifully tended garden deserves a visit. It is surprisingly large for a garden in the middle of a town. Don't miss the corner turned into a dogs' cemetery for many of Henry James faithful companions.

Continue south along West Street to reach Rye Parish Church dedicated to St Mary. It is full of literary associations. Two beautiful windows were donated by E.F.Benson. The West Window over the Font dates from 1933 and is in memory of his parents, Archbishop and Mrs Benson. It is a traditional nativity scene with one exception. One's eye is caught immediately by a small black dog in the foreground. This is Taffy, Benson's beloved Welsh Collie, whom the artist was persuaded to immortalise.

Outside the church are The Quarter Boys on the church tower.

Church with The Quarter Boys above the clock

Like many things in Rye they have their own idiosyncratic way of working. They do not strike on the hour, like most church clocks, but on the quarter. They are actually fibre glass replacements. The originals now stand in the first window of the Clare Chapel on the left of the entrance. A group of interested onlookers usually gathers to hear them chime.

Fletcher's Tea Room in Lion Street is virtually next door to the church. It is the former vicarage where **John Fletcher** spent the first two years of his life. Delicious morning coffee, lunches and afternoon teas are to be had here.

Fletcher's House (now tea rooms)

*Plaque between the two front windows
recording some of the associated history*

After this fortifying stop, pick up the circular tour north up East Street to the High Street. Here you will pass Black Boy House. The unusual name derives from the house's history. Charles II (one of whose nicknames was Black Charles) is rumoured to have stayed here. On the 28th of December, 1929 it was bought by **Radclyffe Hall**, author of 'The Well of Loneliness' and her companion, Una Troubridge. They also owned The Forecastle in Hucksteps Row which became the setting for Hall's novel 'The Master of The House'.

Continue west along the High Street to the Martello Bookshop which takes its name from the Martello towers, a significant part of the coastal landscape in this area.

The bookshop has a feast of new and second-hand books, mainly about Rye. Do make sure you buy a copy of the Tilling map on sale here. This simple pocket size guide is a real labour of love by Katharine Stephen on behalf of the Tilling Society in nearby Guestling. It identifies the probable locations of homes and, importantly, shops in Benson's novels and makes the identification of buildings very straightforward, although it must be remembered that most are now private houses.

With this in your hand you may like to retrace the way you have come. High Street and West Street retain their names in Tilling but as already noted, Mermaid Street metamorphoses into Porpoise Street.

Watchbell Street logically appears as Curfew Street and if you then walk along the High Street past the bank (the site of the stationer in Tilling), you will very quickly find yourself back where you started at the Heritage Centre.

TWO DAY VISIT

Today's exploration is further from Hastings and its sister town of St. Leonards. Henry James made this journey from Rye many times. He had considerable affection for Hastings, describing it in 'Portraits of Places' (1883): "There amid the little shops and the little libraries, the bath chairs and the German bands, the Parade and the long Pier, with a mild climate, a moderate scale of prices and the consciousness of a high civilisation, I should enjoy a seclusion which would have nothing primitive or crude". Were he to return today he would find Hastings somewhat changed, although the fish and chip shops and tattoo parlours bring their own vitality to the town. St Leonards still retains its dignified old world charm.

Leave Rye by the A259. It's a twelve mile route which passes by Winchelsea and through Icklesham and Guestling, entering the Hastings built up area at Ore. From there it is a two mile drive along the Old London Road (as the A259 is called here) to the sea. This is Hastings Old Town, with its ancient cottages and streets and its net towers, in which the fishing nets are dried.

The Old Town area, which has many literary associations, can seem a dauntingly confusing maze of winding streets to the motorist but in fact your sightseeing is very straightforward. When the A259 meets the sea it veers strongly to the right, as for the next two miles it becomes the Hastings and St Leonards seafront, although it does change its name several times along the way. On the literary trail there are four excursions off the seafront, all involving a right hand turn up a road and all lead to a literary site.

The first road off to the right is High Street and is about a hundred metres from the point where the A259 meets the sea. Here, on the left hand side, is St Clement's Church where the poet and painter **Dante Gabriel Rossetti** married Lizzie Siddal, the model for many Pre Raphaelite portraits, in 1860. The sanctuary light and the framed sonnet on the west wall were given to the church in Rossetti's memory. Continuing up the High Street, on the right hand side, at number 5, is a blue plaque on a very pretty house commemorating an earlier stay by Lizzie Siddal in Hastings in 1854.

If you are driving you will have realised (hopefully!) that this is a one way system. Turn right where the High Street meets the A259. **Coventry Patmore** lived in the Mansion House where the two roads meet. He was the chief benefactor of the Roman Catholic Church of Our Lady Star of the Sea on Old London Road (i.e. the A259). Continue right along this road and retrace your earlier route into the town.

Notice the Cutter Hotel at 12 East Parade. Rossetti lodged in this building, in what is now the Saloon Bar, in 1854. Lizzie Siddal was conveniently close by.

Cutter Hotel

The second right hand turn is half a mile along the seafront. After the roundabout, turn right into Albert Road and then immediately into Castle Hill. After 400 metres turn left into Milward Road where, at number 115, is a memorial to **Robert Tressell** who lived in the top flat between 1903 and 1905.

Flat where he lived

Plaque to Robert Tressell on the wall

This is not a conventional blue plaque but one much more fitted to a champion of the working man. A roughly hewn stone commemorates a 'HOUSEPAINTER AND SIGN WRITER AND AUTHOR OF THE RAGGED TROUSERED PHILANTHROPISTS'.

Back now to the seafront by the same route and then continue along the A259 for a shade over one mile to the Royal Victoria Hotel in Saint Leonards on Sea. St Leonards is a very different place from its twin resort of Hastings.

The new town of St Leonards was founded in the 1820s by fashionable London architects James and Decimus Burton, a father and son team. It was the first planned seaside resort in England and its elegant splendour was designed to appeal specifically to a rich and discerning clientele. Some people believe that **Jane Austen's** unfinished novel 'Sanditon' was set here. 'Some people' are seriously deluded as Jane died in 1817 and would hardly have known of the place.

The Royal Victoria Hotel is a very handsome stuccoed brick building built in classical style. Turn right into Maze Hill and St Leonard's Gardens lie immediately behind the hotel. If you park on the sea front this informal tranquil area of lakes and lawns makes a very pleasant walk.

If driving, Maze Hill circles the gardens and goes north to the castellated gatehouse of North Lodge built in 1830. It was here that **Rider Haggard** spent many winters staying at his brother's house, writing in the room above the archway across the road. A blue plaque records the writer's visits but the lodge is now private property and not open to the public.

The fourth and final right hand turn involves some detective work and also some imaginative recreation of earlier times. Bo Peep village, the site of **John Keats'** romance with Isabella Jones, has now been swallowed up by the westward expansion of Hastings and St Leonards and nothing now remains of Keats' rural retreat from London.

If you continue your drive along the A259 for three quarters of a mile to the outskirts of the town, West Marina, you may be pleased to see a public house called The Bo Peep behind which are more recent houses in Keats Close. Hastings West Station here is on the site of the New England Tavern where the poet stayed. To find this station turn right into West Essenden Road and then left into St Vincent's Road.

It's time now to leave Hastings and St Leonards. Rejoin the A259, turning left and retracing your route along the seafront. Pass the Royal Victoria Hotel and 500 metres beyond turn left on to the A21, signposted London and passing Christ Church, so much associated with Sheila Kaye Smith and her husband. This leads directly after three miles to the A2100 and then six miles later to Battle.

William, Duke of Normandy made a solemn vow when he became the conqueror that he would build an abbey on the very spot where he believed God had aided him to conquer England. The High Altar was built over the spot where King Harold fell. Battle Abbey itself was finally consecrated in 1095 when William II presented his father's sword, used to ensure victory, to the abbey. And so finally back to Rye.

CAN I DO THESE TOURS WITHOUT A CAR?

There are mainline direct rail services from London Victoria and London Charing Cross to Hastings, with a connection there for Rye. In fact, exploration is probably a lot easier on foot in both places without the hassle of looking for parking places. There are also direct trains from Hastings to Battle to see the site of the Battle of Hastings.

In Rye bicycles can be hired for the day at the Rye Cycle Hire Shop 01797 223033 (www.visitrye.co.uk).

For those who are really energetic, the 1066 Country Walk (www.1066country.com), which spans 31 miles is a fascinating way to see the area and combines literary and historical sites. It begins at the Norman landing site at Pevensey and moves on through Battle and Hastings to end at Rye. Each town en route has a wealth of accommodation to rest tired legs.

If you are coming by private yacht (or rowing boat!), the Harbour of Rye is open to visiting boats. Just contact the harbour office on 01797 225225 or rye.harbour@environment-agency.gov.uk.

BEST TIME TO VISIT

Many visitors choose to come during the second and third weeks in September for the Rye Arts Festival. There is a very full programme of talks and exhibitions. Full details are to be had from Rye Tourist information Centre at www.visitrye.co.uk.

The most famous date in English history is surely the 14th of October 1066. There is an annual re-enactment of the battle on the weekend closest to the date on the very site where it took place. Further details of events can be found by visiting www.english-heritage.org.uk.

IF YOU HAVE CHILDREN

It may prove difficult (even with the help of superb tea shops) to keep children happy and co operative while you track down all Benson's references to Rye/Tilling.

Use a promised visit to Rye Castle Museum (and its Ypres Tower) as bribery (www./ryemuseum.co.uk). Blood thirsty youngsters can explore the turrets and see where prisoners were chained. Also worth a visit is

Rye Heritage Centre with its unique Rye town model and its sound and light show, 'The Story of Rye'.

On the upper floor of the building is an exhibition of 'penny in the slot' machines from 1900 to 1960 all still in working order. They are operated with old currency pennies which ceased circulation in 1971 but are still readily available at the Heritage Centre. They prove a great hit with children, especially on a rainy afternoon.

Possibly for slightly older children, Rye Heritage Centre has personal handsets on Rye's History and Rye's Ghostly Tales to carry through the streets.

Hastings is a children's paradise. The West Hill Cliff Railway from the High Street or George Street goes up the hill to Smugglers Adventure in St Clement Caves (open dailyfrom10am). Sound effects and 70 life size characters recreate Hastings illegal and highly profitable past (www. smugglersadventure.co.uk). Close by within a medieval siege tent in the grounds of Hastings Castle, the 1066 Story uses projected images, lighting and sound effects to recreate the battle (www.discoverhastings. co.uk).

On the delightfully named Rock-A-Nore Road on Hastings East Hill is Bluereef Aquarium (www.bluereefaquarium.co.uk), giving close encounters with many sea creatures including sea horses octopus and sharks.

THE WEALD and ASHDOWN FOREST

The Enchanted Places

———⊷◈⊶———

WRITERS OF THE WEALD

If you go down to the woods (forest) today you're in for a big surprise. Not only did Winnie the Pooh and his friends live in Ashdown Forest, so too did many other famous writers.

A.A.Milne (1882-1956)

Alan Alexander Milne was appointed Assistant Editor of Punch when only 24 and subsequently also built up a successful literary career. One play in particular, 'Mr Pim Passes By', with Lesley Howard in the title role, had great success both in London and New York.

Had there not been the arrival of the Milnes' only child Christopher Robin in 1920, it is probable that he would merit only a brief entry in literary history but the boy wanted to hear stories about his toy animals. It later became apparent that that was what the reading public wanted as well. Milne really did not want to waste his time, as he saw it, in writing childish whimsy and he was later to admit: "I am not inordinately fond of or interested in children". Even more significantly, Christopher Milne said later that his father had no talent for amusing children or playing with them.

Winnie the Pooh first met the public in a poem printed in Punch magazine in 1924 then reprinted later in the same year in Milne's collection of poetry for children 'When We Were Very Young'.

That was a significant year for the Milne family. Alan and his wife found the 'country cottage' they were looking for in East Sussex that summer. It was in fact a 16th century farmhouse known as Cotchford Farm, outside Hartfield on the edge of Ashdown Forest.

The family drove down from their house in Chelsea to spend weekends and holidays in Sussex, Christopher Robin sitting on his Nanny's knee in the back of the blue car, no doubt clutching his favourite teddy bear and one or two other toy animals, a stripy tiger perhaps and a donkey (today they are all housed in the New York Public Library, except Roo, who has strangely disappeared).

There followed a period of extraordinary output. 'Winnie the Pooh' appeared in 1926. 'Now We Are Six' in 1927 and 'House at Pooh Corner' in 1928. By the time this last Pooh story was published, simultaneously in London and New York, the sales of its predecessors had broken all records. All are set in Ashdown Forest and Milne and E. H. Shephard were both very careful to seek out the appropriate settings in the forest for the stories.

In 1929 nine year old Christopher Robin went off to boarding school and Nanny left to get married. The amazing series of children's books came to an end. Milne felt this was the moment to turn his attention away from children's writing to something much more real and gritty for adults. But what the public wanted, but did not get, were more stories from the House at Pooh Corner.

In 1940 the Chelsea house was sold and the Milnes moved permanently to Cochford Farm. Much of what we know about life there, especially about the early days of the family's residence, comes from Christopher Milne's 'The Enchanted Places', which he wrote in 1947 when he was 27.

Reading the tales of Christopher Robin and Pooh, it is easy to picture an idyllic childhood filled with cosy domesticity. It therefore comes as a shock to the reader to discover the reverse was the case. His unhappy autobiography documents the emotional abuse he suffered when he became identified as the 'real' Christopher Robin. Ironically, he became even better known as a result of this and two later autobiographies.

Many would seek him out in his bookshop in Devon, perhaps thinking the magic of The Hundred Acre Wood would become more real if they could only shake his hand.

In the course of time he saw very little of his father, who suffered a stroke in 1952. Milne died in 1956 but after attending his memorial service, Christopher steadfastly refused to have anything more to do with his mother. He distanced himself from the growing Pooh empire and the copyrights were sold by his mother, Daphne Milne, to the Disney Corporation in 1961. The Corporation has taken its responsibilities very seriously as guardian of a literary heritage and in 1999 paid for the repairs to Possingford bridge (Poohsticks Bridge).

Poohsticks Bridge

Winnie the Pooh (1924-1929 but, in truth, immortal)

Christopher Robin's teddy bear (a present for his first birthday) was originally christened, like so many teddies before and since, Edward Bear. He was renamed Winnie after a Canadian black bear called Winnipeg, the mascot of the Royal Winnipeg Rifles during the First World War, who spent his final years in London Zoo. There is also a very important third bear to consider. E.H.Shephard took his inspiration for his iconic drawings from his own daughter's teddy bear, Growler. Perhaps the bear of little brain should really be called Winnie the Growler. It doesn't sound right does it?

W.B.Yeats (1865-1939) and Ezra Pound (1885-1972)

W. B. Yeats and Ezra Pound spent three winters from 1913 to 1916 sharing Stone Cottage at Coleman's Hatch on the northern edge of Ashdown Forest. Irishman William Butler Yeats was 48 years old and already well known for his poetry and plays whereas the American, Ezra Pound, was 20 years younger and yet to achieve his later wide reputation, even though at that time he was already publishing a book of poetry almost every year. He was however quite a well known figure in literary circles. His role was to act as 'Uncle William's' (as he affectionately called him) secretary.

By this time Yeats had problems reading as he had almost lost the sight in his left eye and his right eye was also very weak. Pound was certainly unenthusiastic about the location in which he found himself, as can be seen in one of his letters to his mother: "My stay in Stone Cottage will not be in the least profitable. I detest the country. Yeats will amuse me part of the time and bore me to death with psychical research the rest. I regard the visit as a duty to posterity".

They both married while in Sussex. Pound was the first, marrying the auspiciously surnamed Dorothy Shakespear, the daughter of Kensington friends. She does not seem to have had her husband's qualms about sharing living space with Yeats and moved in happily to Stone Cottage. Not far from Stone Cottage stands a larger house, 'The Prelude' (now, as it stands at the end of the track, appropriately renamed 'End House'), the family home of Georgie Hyde-Lees. After his long unsuccessful courtship of the Irish beauty Maude Gonne, Yeats married Georgie, the girl next door. Pound was best man at the wedding and part of the honeymoon was spent at Stone Cottage and part at Ashdown Forest Hotel in Forest Row.

After the Sussex interlude their ways parted. Yeats went on to Oxford and then back to Ireland. Pound travelled farther away, first to Paris and subsequently to Ireland.

Sir Arthur Conan Doyle (1859-1930)

Conan Doyle was already famous as the creator of Sherlock Holmes when he moved to Little Windlesham on Hurtis Hill, Crowborough with his second wife Jean, in 1907. His first wife had died the previous year. One attraction of the five gabled houses with its extensive views over the Sussex Downs was to be closer to Jean's family.

He immediately changed the name to the much grander sounding Windlesham Manor, enlarging it considerably by building a billiards room which extended the full width of the house with a large window at each end. At weekends the house was full of distinguished visitors, many travelling down from London but some coming from much closer. Kipling frequently drove over from nearby Burwash.

Sherlock Holmes (improbably first named Sheringford Holmes and sounding more like a country railway station than a great detective) first appeared in 1887 in a 'Study in Scarlet' when Conan Doyle, still a medical doctor like Dr. Watson, was living in Southsea. His investigations continued to be documented during the Windlesham years.

Depending on the time of year, Conan Doyle wrote either in the summerhouse in the garden or in his first floor study. In his story 'The Poison Bell' he describes the view from his study across Crowborough Common to distant Rotherfield. In 'The Valley of Fear', Holmes investigates a murder in Biristone Manor a 'Jacobean brick house' which "rose upon the ruins of the feudal castle" surrounded by "an old fashioned garden of cut yews" on the "fringe of the great Weald Forest". All the evidence points to Groombridge Place, which Conan Doyle visited often. There he would take part in séances with the owners Louisa and Eliza Saint.

Sussex is the setting for three other Holmes stories: 'The Five Orange Pips', 'The Musgrave Ritual' and 'The Sussex Vampire' and at the end of his life the great detective is said to be in retirement on the Sussex coast.

Conan Doyle died in 1930 and was buried in the rose garden of Windlesham Manor. A headstone of English oak was erected with the words "Steel true, blade straight". Jean died ten years later and was buried with him. Subsequently the house became a Residential Care Home and their remains were transferred to Minstead churchyard in Hampshire. Windlesham Manor is privately owned and closed to the public.

Rudyard Kipling (1865-1936)

This most English of writers (although born in Bombay) came to Sussex in 1895, when he and his American wife Caroline (known to all as Carrie), with their two daughters Josephine and Elsie, were newly returned from India via America. They first lived in the pretty village of Rottingdean, outside Brighton, close to the author's uncle, Edward Burne-Jones, the painter. What the Kiplings had not bargained for was the price of his growing literary fame. By 1900 he was the most famous writer of the English speaking world.

The house became the focus for day trippers from Brighton. You, of course, would not be reading this book if you did not share their curiosity about the lives of the famous. Tracing the haunts of the long dead is one thing, harassing the living is far less excusable.

There was another tragic reason to move from Rottingdean. While on a visit to American relations in 1899 their eldest daughter Josephine caught pneumonia and died. The family home was far too full of poignant memories of the child. The Kiplings, now with a son, John, needed an isolated house to mourn in private and Bateman's, outside Burwash, filled that need to perfection (see the Brighton chapter for much more information about Kipling's Rottingdean years).

Kipling was one of the first motoring enthusiasts. In 1900 he bought a Lanchester (which frequently broke down) and he and Carrie were able to combine this love of motoring with house hunting all over Sussex. It was love at first sight when they first saw Bateman's: "a real house in which to settle down for keeps" said Kipling and that is what he proceeded to do.

Batemans

They bought the 17th century former ironmaster's house in 1902 for £9,300. Kipling was then 36 and proceeded to live there until his death in 1936. Carrie remained in the house for 3 more years before her own death in 1939, after which it was left to the National Trust on condition that Kipling's study should remain exactly as it was. It is one of the loveliest houses owned by the Trust, although both the writer Hugh Walpole and Elsie Kipling remembered it as being cold and uncomfortable.

As with any family house, but even more so than most, Bateman's witnessed many highs and lows. Mourning Josephine the family certainly were, but in the early years the house was filled with a good deal of fun and laughter from the two remaining children. Kipling built a pond for them in the grounds with a paddle boat for friends and family. The visitors' book can still be seen in the Library. If a name has F.I.P. beside it the unfortunate guest had fallen in the pond!

Bateman's and the surrounding Weald were a source of inspiration and it was here that the particular Sussex stories were written, notably Puck of Pook's Hill. Traditionally, Pook's Hill is the wooded hilltop which can be seen from his study window.

In 1907 Kipling became the first English writer, and one of the youngest, to be awarded the Nobel Prize for Literature. The £7,700 prize money went towards laying out the Rose Garden and improving the pond.

But there were devastatingly sad times to come. On the outbreak of the First World War, John Kipling was still a week short of his 17th birthday. Desperate to join up, perhaps to prove himself to his father, he had to face rejection from both the Army and the Navy because of his poor eyesight. In future years Kipling would never forgive himself for pulling strings at the highest level, persuading Lord Roberts to give his son a commission in the Irish Guards.

On the 22nd September 1915, aged just 18, the myopic John led his men over the top for the first and last time. His body was never recovered and a gloom settled on Bateman's. Their one surviving child, Elsie, married one of her brother's fellow officers in 1924 and a further sadness for Kipling was that this marriage did not produce any grandchildren.

ONE DAY VISIT

The Winnie the Pooh Trail, with a brief diversion to see Yeats' and Pound's Stone Cottage, centres round the village of Hartfield and a large part of it is best covered on foot. A good place to begin and end your day would be the small town of Forest Row.

You may be put off walking by the word 'Forest'. Don't be. In this case it is actually a mixture of woodland and open heathland. The name derives from its use as a Royal hunting ground in times gone by and this history is reflected in several place names. The original forest was surrounded by a 'pale' or ditch and bank which allowed deer to enter but not leave. People, on the other hand, could pass through the pale at 'hatches' (on foot) or 'gates' (with livestock).

Today place names such as Coleman's Hatch and Chelwood Gate reflect these earlier times. If you do come by car you will find plenty of car parks but do watch out for deer. Many are killed on the forest's roads every year.

Start at Forest Row where the town sign actually advertises itself as being 'The Gateway to Ashdown Forest'. Take the A22 South for 2 miles to Wych Cross and at the crossroads turn left down the Coleman Hatch Road. One mile down the road on the left hand side is the Ashdown Forest Centre. There could not be a better place to get your bearings. Even if you have already armed yourself with the appropriate OS Explorer Map 135 for the area, go to the Information Barn where you will find the maps, leaflets and books on offer are just what you need. There is an excellent small exhibition showing the history of the area and the staff are very helpful. Perhaps even more importantly, the only public toilets in the forest are situated here.

Turn left out of the Car Park and rejoin the Coleman's Hatch Road for approximately 2.5 miles. Before reaching the Hatch public house, there is a narrow road through the woods on the right hand side of the main road with a white board listing the names of cottages along its route. Yeats' and Pound's 'Stone Cottage' is on the left and the 'Prelude' (now more suitably named 'End House') is at the far end. Both are privately owned.

'Coleman's Hatch' was also home to **Christopher Fry (1907 -2005)**. The newly married Christopher and his wife moved to an old mill-house in the village in 1936. The schoolmaster Fry had already gained some reputation in amateur theatricals when the local vicar asked him to write a play for the church's jubilee. The result was 'The Boy with a Cart' to be followed by the highly successful 'The Lady's Not For Burning'. Fry later moved to East Dean near Chichester where he built up very strong links with the Chichester Festival Theatre (see the Chichester chapter)

Now you are ready for Pooh Country.

Return to the Coleman Hatch Road and turn right. Almost immediately you will pass the Hatch public house, with the B2110 sign posted Hartfield on your right. After 2.5 miles you will have reached Hartfield, with Pooh Corner shop and Piglet's Tea-room.

Pooh Corner Shop and Piglet's Tea Room

In the 1920s it was the village sweet shop whither the young Christopher Robin, on the back of his donkey Jessica, was taken the half mile trip from Cotchford Farm every week by his Nanny to spend his pocket money. This utterly delightful shop and café is packed with Pooh memorabilia (it even has the rules for Pooh Sticks in Japanese!). It is the best source for maps of Pooh Country. We especially recommend 'Two Expotitions to The Enchanted Places' by Mike Ridley, the shop's original creator. You'll find it open everyday except Christmas Day and Boxing Day.

We suggest a Cream Tea before you start (Pooh would not worry about having teatime in the morning) but you will have to choose between the Piglet Cream Tea with one scone and the Pooh with two! You will also need to buy an Expotition Certificate to cross off the sites as you visit them. On your return to Pooh Corner you can then have it endorsed with a gold sticker and so become 'certified'!

From Hartfield village take the left fork B2026 signposted to Maresfield. If you glance to your right after about a mile you should be able to catch a glimpse of Cotchford Farm.

It is a private house and not open to the public. After approximately half a mile you will see the signpost of the small village of Chuck Hatch and about 500 metres after that the signpost to Marsh Green and Newbridge. Turn right here down Chuck Hatch Lane and the Pooh Car Park is almost immediately on your right. The walk to Poohsticks Bridge should take about 20 minutes. Do remember to pick up your Poohsticks on the way!

Be warned, in wet weather the walk can be very muddy. Afterwards, when reunited with your car, return to the B2026, turning right towards Maresfield and Uckfield. Continue south a further mile to Gills Lap Car Park. This is the Galleon's Leap of the stories. The Enchanted Place is clearly signposted and is much easier to reach than Poohsticks Bridge. Ten minutes at normal walking speed will bring you there with a further three or four minute stroll to the memorial erected in 1979 to commemorate A.A. Milne and E.H.Shephard who "captured the magic of Ashdown Forest and gave it to the world".

Also nearby is the Sandy Pit. Across the B2026 is The Five Hundred Acre Wood (which became the '100 Aker Wood'). The North Pole and Eeyore's Sad and Gloomy Place have yet to be positively identified but much pleasure can be had in following the clues and doing your own detective work.

The B2026 joins the B 2110 at Gill's Lap. Drive north for 3 miles and you will be back where you started from in Forest Row.

Memorial to Milne and Shephard

TWO DAY VISIT

Today is given over to a thorough exploration of Rudyard Kipling's life at Bateman's (TN19 7DS). If you are making your centre at Forest Row take the A22 south to Maresfield joining the easterly A272 just north of Uckfield. Join the A265 at Heathfield. Remain on this road and Bateman's is ½ mile south of Burwash.

Apart from the house interior, which is kept much as it was in Kipling's time, there are beautiful grounds running down to the small River Dudwell, a restored watermill which grinds corn and Kipling's 1928 Rolls Royce in the garage. The National Trust shop has the largest collection of Kipling books for sale in the area and the Mulberry Tea-room is not to be missed. Bateman's is open from mid-March until the end of October but closed on Thursdays and Fridays.

ONE MORE DAY

There is so much to see and do in this area you may want to extend your visit.

A Conan Doyle Trail could take in an exterior view of the writer's home outside Crowborough and some time exploring Groombridge Place Gardens the probable setting for 'The Valley of Fear'. You'll meet other writers on the way too.

Much depends on how much time you spend on the Winnie the Pooh Trail. If you polish it off in a morning then you are in the right area to investigate the great detective. Otherwise an extra day is well worth while.

From Hartfield take the A2110 for approximately one mile to Groombridge (TN3 9QG.) right on the Sussex/Kent border. The Gardens (rumoured to have been designed in part by **John Evelyn**) and Enchanted Forest are open every day from 10.00am to 5.30pm from mid March to the beginning of November. Although the house itself is closed to visitors there are two small buildings to look out for.

One reproduces Sherlock Holmes' Baker Street study whilst elsewhere in the Gardens is a small exhibition centre filled with memorabilia of recent films shot here, including 'Pride and Prejudice' and Peter Greenway's 'The Draughtsman's Contract'.

Five hundred years ago this was the home of the Waller family. The poet **Edmund Waller** stayed with his relations here while unsuccessfully wooing Lady Dorothy Sidney (fair Sacharissa in the poems) at Penshurst Place. As you walk through the grounds make sure you have a copy of Conan Doyle's 'The Valley of Fear' in your hand to identify the scene of the crime where "the only approach to the house was over a drawbridge" across "a beautiful broad moat".

Leave Groombridge Place and turn immediately left for 100 metres. At the roundabout take the first turning into Station Road, signposted Eridge. Veer to the right after a mile and follow a pretty winding lane with overhanging trees. After two and a half miles join the A26 at Eridge Green, just after the station and turn right for Crowborough. The town sign proudly proclaims it was the home of **Conan Doyle.**

Continuing on the A26, drive through the centre of Crowborough Just before Crowborough Camp turn left into Sheep Plain Road, signposted Jarvis Brooke. Drive across the golf course on Crowborough Common for almost a mile until you reach the junction with Highbrow Road. On your left hand side is the drive to Windlesham Manor (now a private Care Home). There is a commemorative plaque beside the front door.

Rejoin the A26. Turn left and continue along the road you were following. You will pass Barnsgate Manor Vineyard reaching Heron's Ghyll after two miles. Here is Temple Grove, once a prep school but now private housing. The house itself belonged to the Victorian poet, **Coventry Patmore**, most famous probably for his poem 'The Angel in the House', in praise of the wife who knows her place!

Continue along the A26 and at the second roundabout turn right onto the A22 following signs to Haywards Heath (A275). These signs to Haywards Heath at the next roundabout will take you onto the A272. Drive through Piltdown village, which was the home of a very famous piece of fiction in 1921 when a supposedly 150,000 year old skull was discovered here, perhaps the missing link between man and apes. It was not until 1953 that tests proved that not only was the skull a third of the age originally believed but the lower jaw and a tooth belonged to a modern ape.

Which practical joker, living in the area in the 1920s, successfully fooled the whole archaeological world? Many candidates have been put forward, including the main subject of today's literary trail, Conan Doyle himself. The local pub, The Piltdown Man, has a nice representation of the fossilised skull on its sign, with some old photographs in the bar. Children love its large adventure playground.

If you have pony mad youngsters with you, you may want to continue along the A272 to Haywards Heath (it has some pleasant shops too). **Anna Sewell (1820-1878)** wrote part of her only novel 'Black Beauty' while living here. It was published three months before her death. At the entrance to the town take the B2112, signposted Lindfield and then take the second turning on the right named New England Road. A blue plaque on the wall of Heyworth Primary School marks her former home and the school incorporates a black horse in its badge.

Retrace your journey and half a mile beyond Piltdown turn left to Fletching, the burial place of **Edward Gibbon (1737-1794)**. The historian and author gained the patronage of John Baker Holroyd, later

Lord Sheffield of Sheffield Park and spent nine months of 1787 there, completing 'The Decline and Fall of The Roman Empire'. The church is easily found at the end of the village High Street with the magnificent Holroyd family mausoleum on the left hand side of the altar. After all this exploring you may be hungry. It's well worth hunting out The Griffin in the High Street. It's one of the nicest gourmet pubs in the area.

Well fortified, continue north past Sheffield Park and so through the familiar territory now of Chelwood Gate, Wych Cross and back to Forest Row.

CAN I DO THESE TOURS WITHOUT A CAR?

Much of this exploration is best done while walking. Once you are in the area begin at Hartfield and tackle the whole Winnie the Pooh Trail on foot. Rudyard Kipling's home at Bateman's is also accessible by public transport.

Bus No.318 from Uckfield goes to Etchingham Station. From there it is a 3 mile taxi ride to Bateman's.

BEST TIME TO VISIT

It is so difficult to pick out a best time to see the Forest. Every season has its own beauty although it is obviously busiest in summer.

You may also want to check the dates for the South of England Show held every year at the beginning of June at the South of England Showground in Ardingly, on the B2028, approximately 3 miles west of Forest Row.

IF YOU HAVE CHILDREN

Most children will be in heaven at the thought of following the Pooh Trail, although be warned. The walk to Pooh Sticks Bridge can be very muddy in wet weather. The route back to the car park is uphill and may be a challenge to little legs. It is certainly difficult for pushchairs.

Approximately three miles south of Forest Row on the A275 at

Sheffield Park Station is the Bluebell Railway (www.bluebellrailway.co.uk). Enthusiastic volunteers run a frequent steam train service on this five mile stretch of line. As the name suggests it is particularly lovely in Spring as it runs through a bluebell valley. Many film and TV sequences have been shot here.

If there are adults in the party who may become restless with all this talk of stuffed toys there are other nearby attractions which will keep them amused all day.

Look out for the Kent and Sussex Apple Juice and Cider Centre (open Tuesday - Sunday 10am to 5pm) on the Edenbridge road in Hartfield.

(www.perryhillorchards.co.uk)

The Ashdown Forest Llama Park in Wych Cross (open daily 10 00am -5 00pm) is well worth a visit. The shop is full of luxurious alpaca knitwear and South American crafts. In addition to an adventure play area and coffee shop the park also offers the chance for an unusual day out walking with llamas through Ashdown Forest. Participants must be over 14 (www.llamapark.co.uk).

INDEX

Dickens Charles, 11
Dilke Charles, 21
Douglas Keith, 59
Doyle Arthur Conan, 65, 122-123, 130-131
Eliot T.S., 37-38, 42, 81
Engels Friedrich, 43, 46
Evelyn John, 85
Farjeon Eleanor, 69, 71
Fitzalan Richard, 28
Fletcher John, 97, 109-110
Fletcher Revd. Richard, 97
Forster E.M., 36, 44, 81
Foyle Gilbert, 42
Fry Christopher, 27, 126-127
Fry Roger, 79
Galsworthy John, 68-69
Garnet David, 79
Garnett Eve, 84
George IV (Prince Regent), 1, 13, 18, 84
Gibbon Edward, 131-132
Gibbons Stella, 18-19
Godden Rumer, 40, 44, 98, 100-101
Grant Duncan, 79, 82, 90
Grenfell Henry, 45
Greene Graham, 6-7, 9-10, 13
Haggard Rider, 104, 115
Hall Radclyffe, 111
Hamilton Patrick, 8, 10, 12
Harvard John, 88, 89
Hayley William, 22-23, 29, 31
Heyer Georgette, 57-58, 67
Hornung E.W., 65
Hudson W.H., 18
Huxley Aldous, 81
Huxley Thomas, 38, 44

James Cornelia, 9
James Henry, 98-99, 109, 111
James Peter, 9
Jefferies Richard, 18
Johnson Dr.Samuel, 2, 3, 10-11
Jones Isabella, 21, 115
Jones Peter, 6, 91
Jones Sir Roderick, 5
Jourdain Margaret, 7
Kaye-Smith Sheila, 19, 100, 102-103, 105-106, 115
Keats John, 21-22, 28-30, 63, 103, 115
Keats Tom, 21
Keynes Maynard, 79-80, 91
Kipling Carrie, 3, 4, 123-125
Kipling Elsie, 4, 123, 125
Kipling John, 3, 16, 124 – 125
Kipling Josephine, 4, 123
Kipling Rudyard, 3-4, 14-15, 58, 123-125, 129
Lacy Mary, 29
Lamb Charles, 35, 59
Lamb Mary, 35
Larkin Philip, 28
Lawrence D.H., 60, 71
Lear Edward, 45
Lopokova Lydia, 79-80
Lowry Malcolm, 90, 108
Lowry Margerie, 90
Lyall Edna, 42
MacInnes Colin, 8
MacInnes Lancelot, 8
Mansfield Katherine, 4-5
Marx Karl, vii, 43
Maxwell Gavin, 36
McCartney Paul, 106
Meynell Alice, 60, 71